The 100 Deadliest Female Serial Killers

Mason Ryan

Other books by Mason Ryan:

Everything You Always Wanted To Know About Serial Killers
(But Were Afraid To Ask)

The 100 Deadliest Serial Killers

CONTENTS

INTRODUCTION

The media sometimes give one the impression that violence and murder has always been the preserve of men but that's not actually true at all. As this book will illustrate, all human beings - regardless of their gender - are capable of evil and the most awful crimes. A number of crime authors think (with some justification you might argue) that female serial killers have not received half as much ink as their male counterparts. Because of this we sometimes forget just how many female killers there have been down the decades and centuries. Take someone like Roberta Elder for example. Elder killed over fourteen people (including children) in the 1950s by way of poison but there is little information about her and many people have probably never heard of her. Because she was black and her victims were black the story of Roberta Elder received little press coverage at the time and she was sort of forgotten. By any standards though a killer capable of killing at least fourteen people is prolific and deadly.

It has been estimated that around 15% of serial killers are women but this could well be a very conservative estimate. Psychologist Marissa Harrison concluded from her study that female serial killers were generally motivated by material gain whereas male serial killers were mostly motivated by sexual urges. Well, that's not always the case. We are sometimes, for example, told that there have never been sexually motivated necrophile female serial killers but this simply isn't true. Piroska Jancsó Ladányi was a female serial killer from Hungary who sexually abused the bodies of her female victims. Guadalupe Martínez de Bejarano, a Mexican female serial killer, was also a necrophile. The notorious medical killer Jane Toppan would get into bed with her victims after she killed them because the murders gave her a sexual thrill. Debra Denise Brown, who went on a murderous rampage with a dreadful man named Alton Coleman, was a sadistic rapist, killer, and pedophile.

Female killers are more likely to use poison than their male counterparts and so, we are told, are generally regarded to be less gruesome. 'They're often described as quiet killers,' wrote Discover Magazine of female serial killers. 'They typically don't butcher, nor torture. They prefer poison — in 50 percent of all cases — and smothering to conspicuous knives and guns. They also tend to kill at home or at work, drawing less attention than the random, far-flung sprees common among men. In a 2013 paper analyzing the characteristics of female serial killers, sociologist Amanda Farrell wrote that they kill, on average, over longer stretches of time than their male counterparts.'

Once again though, there are many exceptions. Women can be just as gruesome as male killers. The Czech female serial killer Jaroslava Fabiánová once stabbed a victim over forty times. Lizzie Halliday killed her husband and mutilated his corpse. Carol M. Bundy decapitated one of her victims to get rid of ballistic evidence (she had shot him in the head). Dana Sue Gray stabbed one of her elderly victims in the neck and left the knife there. Irina Gaidamachuk would beat her victims to death with an axe or hammer. Sofia Zhukova, a Russian killer, would kill people with an axe and then dismember their bodies. It is said that Zhukova had internal human organs in her fridge when she was captured. Joanna Dennehy is a female serial killer who stabbed three men to death with a knife in England in 2013 and tried to kill two others. These were brutal and random attacks with no apparent motivation. Female serial killers can be just as violent and just as gruesome as their more famous male counterparts.

Female serial killers are generally more likely to know their victims than male killers. Female serial killers are also more likely to (as we shall see in this book) work in the medical profession in some capacity. Many notorious female killers throughout history have killed babies and children. Female serial killers are much less likely to have prior criminal convictions than male serial killers and this, one might argue, makes it a lot harder to see them coming. There are many female serial killers in history and they come from all backgrounds and all nations. They can be just as deadly and just as dangerous as the most notorious male serial killers. In fact, one might argue that, in many cases, female serial killers have a cunning and nous that their male counterparts don't always seem to possess. They do say the female of the species is deadlier than the male. Well, let's put that to the test. It's time to countdown the 100 deadliest female serial killers in history...

THE LIST - THE 100 DEADLIEST FEMALE SERIAL KILLERS IN HISTORY

(100) SUSANA TOLENDANO & CHELSEA LEE RICHARDSON (Years Active 2003, Two Victims)

Susana Alejandra Toledano and Chelsea Lea Richardson were born in 1984 in Tarrant County, Texas. Along with Chelsea's boyfriend Andrew Wamsley, this duo conspired in the murders of Andrew's parents because Andrew was in line to receive a generous inheritance should they die. Chelsea came from a fairly humble background and was very eager to experience what life might be like with money. The motivation for the murders was heightened by the fact that Andrew's parents had stopped supporting him financially because they didn't approve of his relationship with Chelsea.

Chelsea and Andrew had an accomplice in their murderous scheme in the form of Chelsea's friend Susana Toledano. Susan was completely under the control of her friend Chelsea and was manipulated into taking part in these murders. You could argue that the principal villain (or at the very least the real mastermind) of this case was actually Chelsea Lea Richardson. The trio managed to purchase a gun and on November the 9th 2003 they attacked the Wamsley family - Rick, Suzanna and daughter Sarah. The first murder attempt was rather bungled. Andrew drove into Rick's jeep and then Susan tried to shoot his car gas tank to make it explode. They had got this idea from watching a television show. However, real life is not an episode of The A-Team or Airwolf and the plan didn't work. Susan missed the gas tank when she tried to shoot it.

Chelsea was not involved in the first murder attempt because she wanted to have an alibi. Chelsea was though the manipulative and cold heart of this wicked trio. She was the driving force behind this murderous plan. The trio decided that the best thing to do now would be to murder the Wamsley family in their home. On December the 11th 2003, Rick and Suzanna Wamsley were murdered at their house in Mansfield. Rick Wamsley was shot in the head and stabbed over twenty times. Suzanna Wamsley was also shot in the head and stabbed multiple times. Mercifully, their daughter Sarah was not in the house when the attack occurred.

Susana Toledano had shot Suzanna Wamsley dead while she slept on a sofa. Rick Wamsley heard the shot and rushed out - whereupon Susana shot him too. He still managed to put up a fight though and a struggle for the gun ensued. Chelsea Lea Richardson then got hold of the gun and shot Rick in the back. Susana Tolendo then stabbed Rick multiple times while he was face down on the floor. Susana Toledano was then ordered by Chelsea Lea Richardson to stab Suzanna Wamsley just to make sure she was dead.

Andrew Wamsley, who was present at the murders, then phoned the police to report an incident at the house. A bold move but it was motivated by greed. He simply wanted to get his hands on his inheritance as quickly as possible. The police found a gruesome crime scene when they went to the house. At first they suspected that this was a burglary that had gone wrong. The Wamsley's were, just to further complicate this case, in a witness protection scheme. It was even speculated that a professional hitman had killed them.

Chelsea Lea Richardson had planned in advance for this stage of the crime. She arranged for a man named Jeremy Lavender to provide her with an alibi. This alibi was naturally proven to be false. Sarah Wamsley, who was luckily absent the night of the murders, had a child with a man named Todd Cleveland. Because Sarah and Todd had a famously bitter custody dispute over this child after they split up, Todd Cleveland actually became a suspect in the Wamsley murders but was later (of course) cleared of any involvement.

Sarah, because she was now due for an inheritance too, was also briefly a suspect in the murders of her parents! She had to take a lie detector test for the police to prove her innocence. Sarah was pretty certain that her brother Andrew was involved in the murders and began legal action to block his inheritance. The breakthrough in the case came when hair found in Rick Wamsley's hand was matched to Susana Toledano through DNA tests. Susana Toledano and Andrew Wamsley were both arrested.

Toledano agreed to testify against Chelsea Lea Richardson and Andrew Wamsley to avoid the death penalty. As a consequence she received life in prison. Chelsea Lea Richardson was sentenced to death by lethal injection but in 2011 the sentence was commuted to life in prison. Andrew Wamsley was convicted of capital murder and sentenced to life imprisonment. Hilario Cardenas, who illegally supplied the deadly trio with a gun, also received a prison sentence. One of the knottiest and strangest true crime cases in recent memory was finally at an end.

(99) KARLA FAYE TUCKER (Years Active 1983, Two Victims)

Karla Faye Tucker was born in Houston in 1959. Tucker was convicted of two murders in Texas in 1984 and executed by lethal injection after fourteen years on death row. She was convicted for killing two people with a pickaxe during a burglary. Tucker had a very unconventional and damaging childhood. Her mother was a rock groupie who got Karla involved in prostitution when she was only thirteen. Karla also began drinking and taking drugs at a preposterously young age. Her father left home when she was very young so she had no role models in her life whatsoever. When Karla was only twenty her mother died of a drugs overdose and left her feeling alone in the world.

In the early eighties Karla (then still in her early twenties) spent most of her time with a biker gang (of sorts) and on June the 13th, 1983, Karla and a man named Daniel Ryan Garrett went to the Houston apartment of Jerry Lynn Dean. Karla and Garrett were both off their heads on a variety of drugs and much alcohol. The purpose of their visit was to steal Dean's motorcycle. Dean was the former husband of Karla's best friend and Karla seemed to have a dislike for him (it is said that Dean once destroyed some photographs of Karla's mother).

Jerry Lynn Dean was sleeping when they entered the apartment so Garrett hit him with a hammer. Karla Faye Tucker then finished Dean off by striking him with a pickaxe. The duo then noticed that someone else was in the room. This turned out to be a young woman named Deborah Thornton. Karla attacked Deborah with the pickaxe and struck her several times. Deborah was left dead with the pickaxe still lodged in her body. Karla and Garrett then stole some money and fled. In the space of a few minutes Karla Faye Tucker had brutally slaughtered two people with a pickaxe. She was later recorded on a police wire tap saying that she'd experienced an orgasm each time she'd struck one of the victims with the pickaxe.

The police investigation didn't take too long to deduce that Karla and Garrett were the culprits for this gruesome robbery and they were brought into custody in a matter of weeks. Karla Faye Tucker and Daniel Ryan Garrett were both sentenced to death at the trial which followed (Karla had been advised by her legal team to plead not guilty - which was obviously a mistake). Karla said she didn't even remember that night because she had taken so many drugs. Garrett died of liver disease in 1993 before he could be executed.

Karla Faye Tucker, meanwhile, found God while in prison and a campaign to have her death sentence commuted attracted support from various people and groups including Pope John

Paul II, Newt Gingrich, Bianca Jagger, and the European Parliament. Why all the sympathy for a woman who had brutally killed two innocent people with a pickaxe? If you were being really cynical you might suggest it was because Karla was female, white, and quite interactive. These famous campaigners didn't seem to be offering the same sympathy and support to black male prisoners on death row for similar crimes. Still, it was hard not to at least have some degree of sympathy for Karla. She didn't seem like a monster at all and while most killers conveniently seem to find God in prison she appeared more sincere than most.

Karla wrote a long letter to Texas Governor George W. Bush in which she asked to have her death sentence commuted and expressed her sorrow for what she had done. Karla said she would help rehabilitate other women in prison so that they were better people when they were released. Bush predictably (and rather heartlessly you might suggest) simply ignored this letter and refused to get involved. He didn't really care if a woman was executed or not. Bush had voters to think about and didn't want to be seen to be being soft on crime. Karla Faye Tucker was therefore executed by lethal injection on February the 3rd, 1998. For her last meal, she simply requested a banana, a peach, and a garden salad with ranch dressing.

(98) JASMINE RICHARDSON (Years Active 2006, Three Verified Victims)

Jasmine Richardson is one of the youngest serial killers in history. In Alberta, Canada, in 2006, she helped murder her parents and stabbed her eight year-old brother to death. She was just twelve years-old at the time. Jasmine Richardson was heavily under the influence of her twenty-three year-old boyfriend Jeremy Steinke - a nutty character who claimed to be a werewolf. The motive for the murders was that Richardson was distraught and upset that her family didn't approve of her relationship with Steinke. Of course they didn't approve of the relationship. She was only twelve!

Steinke was naturally deemed to be involved in the murders. This diabolical pair had met through online vampire chat forums. Steinke had proposed marriage to Richardson and she accepted. When her parents (predictably) disapproved she decided to be a full accomplice in the murder of her entire immediate family. Jasmine apparently pretended to be 15 years-old when she met Jeremy Steinke and while that's slightly better than being twelve it didn't make things markedly different. Steinke was still consorting with what he knew must be an underage girl. Just before the murders the pair had apparently watched the Oliver Stone film Natural Born Killers and drawn inspiration from the serial killer movie.

Steinke, with Jasmine Richardson's help, stabbed her parents and then Jasmine Richardson stabbed her young brother Jacob in the chest. Steinke then slit Jacob's throat. Jacob had begged for his life but they still killed him. Jasmine Richardson said she killed her brother because she felt it would be cruel to let him grow up with no parents. A few hours after these brutal and callous murders, Steinke and Jasmine Richardson were seen laughing and joking together in a diner. Jasmine Richardson said she helped kill her family because she thought it would bring her closer to Steinke. She was clearly mentally ill and highly disturbed.

It obviously didn't take Miss Marple to deduce that Steinke and Jasmine Richardson were responsible for these murders. They were in custody fairly soon. Jasmine Richardson and Jeremy Steinke were both convicted for their crimes. Steinke received three life sentences but Jasmine Richardson, in a move that angered many Canadians, was released after ten years and given a new identity. Because of her age, Jasmine Richardson could be only be convicted of ten years in prison under Canadian law. Society has always struggled to work out what to do with children charged with very adult crimes like murder and manslaughter. It still does.

Jasmine Richardson took a university course near the end of her sentence and was judged by the authorities to have genuine remorse and regret for her crimes. While that may or may not be true it obviously isn't much consolation to the three dead members of her family. Jeremy Steinke, naturally, got a much harsher sentence. They basically locked Steinke up and threw the key away - which doesn't seem unreasonable given the circumstances. He is clearly a highly dangerous and manipulative man. Steinke's friend Kacy Lancaster, who was nineteen at the time of the murders, was charged with being an accessory for driving them away from the scene and helping to remove evidence. She was eventually given a sentence of one year under house arrest.

Jasmine Richardson was released in 2016 and now has her identity protected. The authorities believe she has been completely rehabilitated. You can't help feeling that Jasmine Richardson got a light sentence not simply because of her age but also because of her gender. It hardly seems fair that young Jacob lost his life in brutal fashion yet his sister is now a free woman with most of her life still ahead of her. Whatever happens to Jasmine Richardson now will never erase her infamy. She seems destined to remain Canada's youngest multiple killer for a very long time.

(97) JUDITH NEELLEY (Years Active 1982, Two Victims)

Judith Neelley (born Judith Adams) was born in Murfreesboro, Tennessee, in 1956. She had a rather difficult early life because her father (who was an alcoholic) died when she was nine. When she was fifteen, Judith Neelley met a 26 year-old man named Alvin Howard Neelley. She fell in love and the couple married in 1980 and had children. Alvin Howard Neelley was a despicable man though. He was a sadist, rapist, and murderer. Judith, who wasn't any better herself, conspired in his awful crimes and seemed to enjoy them as much as he did.

This twisted couple staged a number of armed robberies (even when Judith Neelley was pregnant) and were pretty much out of control. Judith gave birth to twins while she was detained at the Youth Development Center in Rome, Georgia. This youth center suffered a number of alarming incidents later when one employee was shot at and another had a Molotov cocktail thrown at their home. Judith Neelley was obviously suspected of these attacks at the time.

In September 1982, the Neelleys abducted a thirteen year-old girl named Lisa Ann Millican. They took Lisa to a motel where she was raped and kept as a prisoner. Judith Neelley injected Lisa with cleaning fluid in an attempt to kill her but when this did not work she shot her dead. The body of Lisa Ann Millican was thrown off a canyon after her death. Judith Neelley then anonymously called the police and told them where to find the body.

The following week the Neelleys abducted a young couple named Janice Chatman and John Hancock. Janice was raped and killed and although John was shot he managed to survive. John was able to describe his attackers and the Neelleys, after some police surveillance, were arrested. It was then established that Judith Neelley was responsible for the attempted murders of the Youth Development Center employees too. That news probably didn't come as a great surprise to anyone. Judith Neelley now had two attempted murders to add to her tally of two official murders.

Judith Neelley actually gave birth to her third child while awaiting her trial. What a great start in life that must be - the child of Judith Neelley! Judith Neelley was eventually convicted for the torture and murder of Lisa Ann Millican and sentenced to death. She also confessed to killing Janice Chatman. Alvin Howard Neelley pleaded guilty to murder and assault and evaded the death penalty (he was not charged with Millican's murder - that was his wife's solo handiwork). He ended up with life in prison.

Judith Neelley was only days away from her execution in 1999 when Governor Fob James commuted her sentence to life in prison. Judith Neelley later said she had found God in prison and claimed to pray every day for the family of Lisa Ann Millican. You could probably forgive the family of Lisa Ann Millican if they didn't find that much of a consolation. Though captured fairly soon before she murdered that many people, Judith Neelley was by any standards a sadistic and evil woman responsible for some awful crimes.

(96) CAROLINE GRILLS (Years Active 1947-1953, Four Victims)

Caroline Grills was born in Balmain, New South Wales, Australia in 1888. Killers come in all shapes and sizes and Grills is a classic case in point. You might suggest that she was rather like Australia's own version of Nannie Doss. To the outside world, Grills seemed like a perfectly normal and respectable woman. She married in 1908 and had four sons. Decades later in 1947, Grills became a suspect in the deaths of her 87-year-old stepmother Christine Mickelson; relatives by marriage Angelina Thomas and John Lundberg; and sister in law Mary Anne Mickelson.

The motivation for the murders was presumed to have been financial. Mary Anne Mickelson, for example, had inherited a house from Caroline's father and Caroline obviously presumed that she would be given the house if anything happened to Mary Anne. Grills was a poisoner who used thalium to kill her victims. Thalium, which is odourless and tasteless, used to be widely used a rat poison and was very easy to purchase in stores. Thalium is sometimes called the poisoner's poison.

Caroline Grills would put the thalium in cakes and biscuits she had baked for relatives. One of her other ruses was to slip the poison into a cup of tea she had made for someone. Although the official tally of deaths credited to Grills is four it was established without too much doubt that she also attempted to poison at least three other people. Killers who use poison as a form of murder sometimes tend to become overconfident. They tend to think they have devised a clever and undetectable method of murder but all famous poisoners, just like serial killers who uses guns, knives, or their bare hands, usually get captured in the end.

According to Australia's Dark Heart - 'Throughout 1951-1942 various family members became ill, including Mrs Lundberg, although they suffered with this illness, they all survived. John Downey was one of those whom became ill. He had read a story in a newspaper in October of 1952 about poisonings; this raised his suspicions about 'Aunt Carrie'. He spied her reaching into her apron pocket and then drop something into the cup of tea she was carrying. He had the smarts about him to switch the cups and take a sample of the tea to police. Police tested the sample and found that it contained thallium. This was enough for investigators to examine the deaths of the other members of Grills' family.'

Grills was 63 years-old when she was charged with murder. Bodies were exhumed in this case to establish the guilt of Caroline Grills. A jury took less than twenty minutes to find her guilty. She was initially given a death sentence but this was later relegated to life in prison. Grills became known as Aunt Thally (clever!) in prison. As a consequence of the case, the sale of thalium or products containing thalium was banned in Australia.

Caroline Grills was a rather bewildering presence during the trial and her motivations were never firmly established in any one direction. The prosecutor Mick Rooney QC thought that Grills simply enjoyed killing. He called her "a killer who poisoned for sport, for fun, for the kicks she got out of it, for the hell of it, for the thrill that she and she alone in the world knew the cause of the victims' suffering." Caroline Grills died in 1960 at the age of 71. She was an inmate of Sydney's Long

Bay prison.

(95) MARY ELIZABETH WILSON (Years Active 1955-1957, Four Suspected Victims)

Mary Elizabeth Wilson was born Mary Elizabeth Cassidy in 1889 in Catchgate, Stanley, County Durham. In true crime circles she is known as The Merry Widow of Windy Nook for murdering her husbands. Mary Elizabeth Wilson was a most unlikely serial killer in appearance. She looked like your average run of the mill granny. Her first marriage was in 1914 to a man named John Knowles. The lived in a place called Windy Nook - hence her nickname. Knowles died in 1955 and Mary married again - this time to John Russell. However, Russell died less than two years into the marriage. Mary Elizabeth Wilson had naturally picked up a modest little financial windfall from the death of two husbands in the space of only a couple of years.

In 1957, Mary entered her third marriage when she got hitched to a retired man named Oliver Leonard. This marriage lasted all of twelve days before Oliver Leonard suddenly died. Husband number four was a 76 year-old man named Ernest Wilson. Ernest Wilson was dead within a year of marrying Mary Elizabeth Wilson and Mary happily inherited his house and money. Now, you might think that all these husbands suddenly dropping dead would have attracted more suspicion but apparently the cause of death in each case was cited as natural causes. The medical authorities certainly didn't seem to suspect anything.

The downfall of Mary Elizabeth Wilson was her gallows sense of humour. You might say that Mary rather shot herself in the foot with her own morbid wit. What activated suspicion in her was the jokes she dispensed after these family tragedies. When her third husband died, Mary joked that the sandwiches at the funeral should be saved for the next one. After Ernest Wilson died, Mary is said to have joked to the undertaker that she should get a discount for giving him so much business! This led to much local tittle tattle and innuendo about Mary and the police got involved and eventually exhumed the bodies of two of her husbands. The bodies were found to contain phosphorus. It seems they had been killed by large doses of insect poison.

The day of the planned exhumations, Mary seemed unphased and told the local newspaper - "I am not worried about what they are saying. I can go to the blessed sacrament - I am a Catholic - tomorrow. I take no notice of the tittle-rattle. It is all jealousy. I am not worried at all about what is going on." Despite her (obviously misplaced) optimism and bluster, the 66 year-old Mary was arrested and charged with murder. Mary Elizabeth Wilson always seemed far too cheerful to be a genuine grieving widow and that obviously led to her capture. As far as serial killers go, she was a terrible actor.

The prosecution at the trial found it rather difficult to prove a financial motive for the murders because Mary's husbands were not rich men in the least. In a way that made her crimes worse. She simply seemed to have developed an addiction to killing husbands - despite the somewhat paltry financial benefits these murders netted. Maybe she was simply another one of those serial poisoners who just liked going to funerals. Mary was initially sentenced to death at the trial but this sentence was then downsized to life in prison after an intervention by the Home Secretary. Mary Elizabeth Wilson died in prison in 1963. She was in her early seventies when she passed away.

(94) DOROTHY JEAN MATAJKE (Years Active 1983-1987, 3 Victims)

Dorothy Matajke, born in 1930 and a resident of Nevada, murdered three people by poisoning in Arkansas in 1987. She is (predictably) now known as The Arkansas Poisoner. Matajke worked as a nurse's aide and cared for the elderly. Several of her patients died in suspicious circumstances but she was only convicted of fraud and sentenced to five years in prison. Matajke was very lucky at the time that she was convicted of fraud rather than investigated for murder. The authorities didn't seem to be aware of how serious her crimes really were. Matajke actually escaped from prison but was recaptured in 1980. When her sentence ended she went to Little Rock and (believe it or not) was somehow able to resume her old duties as a carer.

In 1985 she moved in with Paul Kinsey and his wife Opal as their nurse. Paul was 72 and Opal was 71. Matajke was essentially a live in companion. Her duties were to fetch their groceries and prepare their meals and medication. She was also supposed to supply them with companionship and kindness but these two qualities were sorely lacking in the thoroughly heartless Dorothy Matajke. Opal Kinsey suspiciously died a few months after Matajke began her duties. The cause of death was assumed to be cancer. Paul Kinsey wasn't so sure though. He had noticed that the food and medication being served to him by Dorothy Matajke seemed to making him feel worse rather than better.

Kinsey (very sensibly) eventually stopped eating Matajke's food and declined her pills. He then (even more sensibly) fired Dorothy Matajke and booted her out of the house. Matajke had another patient at this time though named Marion Doyle. Doyle was suffering from cancer and died only nine days after Dorothy Matajke started caring for her. At first the authorities thought Doyle might have taken her own life but the plot thickened when they looked into Marion Doyle's finances and saw that a number of cheques from Doyle had gone to Dorothy Matajke. The money ran into the thousands. The signature on the cheques was very suspicious and appeared to have been forged.

The body of Marion Doyle was therefore exhumed and found to contain traces of arsenic. By this time Paul Kinsey, who had also obviously already been poisoned by Dorothy Matajke, was

almost on his death bed. The police searched the home of
Dorothy Matajke and found arsenic. She was charged with first
degree murder in the case of Doyle, and first degree battery in
the case of Kinsey. Kinsey subsequently died in 1987, so
Matajke was charged with first degree murder for the
poisoning of him. In 1987 Matajke - aged 56 - was sentenced
to life for killing Paul Kinsey, and later sentenced to 60 years
for killing Marion Doyle after a plea bargain. Dorothy Matajke
was a very ruthless woman who preyed upon ill and elderly
people purely for financial gain. She was just about the last
person in the world you'd want caring for a relative.

(93) ESTIBALIZ CARRANZA (Years Active 2008-2010, Two Victims)

Estibaliz Carranza, born in Mexico in 1978, is a Spanish-
Mexican woman who became known as The Ice Cream Killer
for two murders she committed in Austria. She moved to
Spain as a child and went to college. Carranza studied
economics at the University of Barcelona. Her father was a
journalist and author. Carranza lived in Germany for a time
and was an intelligent women who spoke different languages.
Red-haired and attractive, Estibaliz Carranza seemed like a
very unlikely killer at first glance.

Carranza eventually helped run an ice cream shop in Vienna
and murdered her husband Holger and later her lover
Manfred because she was frustrated that they hadn't made her
pregnant (by a quirk of fate though she was actually pregnant
by another man at the time of her arrest) and generally tired of
both relationships. Both of the victims were shot in the back of
the head and then cut up with a chainsaw in the apartment
that served as a store room for the Schleckeria ice cream
parlour. The body parts were put in freezers and then
surround by air fresheners to disguise the smell.

After she killed Manfred and cut his body up, Estibaliz
Carranza calmly went out to get a manicure because of the

damage done to her nails. When people inquired about the whereabouts of her husband, Carranza told them he had joined a Hari Krishna sect in India. She later discovered that her husband's decapitated head was stuck to the bottom of the freezer so she poured concrete over it. It was some routine maintenance work in 2011 that discovered the grisly secrets of the ice cream shop. Carranza fled to Italy but was captured several days later.

In custody, Estibaliz Carranza was found, to the surprise of absolutely no one, to be suffering from severe mental disorders. She was deemed to be someone who was highly dangerous and would most likely kill again if she was ever released. In court, the 34 year-old Estibaliz Carranza dabbed at tears and said she could hardly believe what she had done. "I never thought I would be able to go through with it. It was 3pm. There were children outside, it was nice weather, someone must have heard. I thought the police would come. Then my mobile phone rang. It was the ice-cream parlour, saying they needed me to come over." Estibaliz Carranza said she had wanted to burn the bodies but when this proved difficult she used a chainsaw instead. She said she spent many days cleaning the chainsaw afterwards.

Estibaliz Carranza was sentenced to life in a secure mental institution in 2012. She is said to be so dangerous that she is in an institution with men rather than women. Carranza gave birth to a son and got married while in prison. She also wrote a memoir entitled My Two Lives: The Real Story of the Ice Lady. There were even stories that Hollywood was interested in turning her memoir into a film but, as of yet, nothing has come of this.

Of disposing of her husband, Estibaliz Carranza wrote - 'I decided to go to the DIY store, where I purchased a hydraulic lift that the taxi driver helped bring to my front door to help me lift the body into the freezer, but Holger was so heavy that it broke. I then realised I was going to have to cut him into pieces, so I went back there again and purchased a chainsaw. I remember that the salesperson looked at me strangely when I told him I wanted to operate it myself. He told me you better watch out, or blood is going to flow. I thought to myself he didn't know how true that was. I can say to anyone who has seen a horror film that the reality of cutting up a body with a chainsaw is far worse. I put the pieces into the freezer but despite that the smell would not go away. I tried so many different perfume sprays but nothing worked. It was ever present.'

(92) ELIZABETH RIDGEWAY (Years Active 1681–1684, Four Victims)

Elizabeth Ridgeway was born in the late 17th century on a farm outside Ibstock, Leicestershire. Elizabeth lived with her mother for most of her young life. In fact she was nearly thirty when this relationship came to an end. The cause of the split? Well, Elizabeth murdered her mother by means of poison after they had a falling out. She used white mercury or arsenic to poison her victims. You've probably heard of the term mercury poisoning. Elizabeth took mercury poisoning to the next level.

After the death of her mother, Elizabeth had to get a job and ended up becoming a maid in a house not too far way. It is said that she fell out with a fellow servant there and so poisoned him with arsenic. Elizabeth Ridgeway was definitely the last person you'd want to get into an argument with. You could say that she was someone who knew how to hold a grudge! Her method for poisoning someone was the usual one practiced by numerous poisoners through the decades (and indeed centuries). She would slip poison into porridge that someone would eat or simply put some in a cup of tea and give it to the victim.

Elizabeth Ridgeway was said to be an attractive woman and she soon had a number of men vying for her attention. One such man was John King. Elizabeth gave King the impression that she was willing to become his wife but when she decided she didn't want to go through with this she simply poisoned him to rid herself of this problem. In 1683 she married Thomas Ridgeway. Elizabeth had chosen Thomas Ridgeway because he was wealthy. Guess what happened to Thomas Ridgeway? That's right. Death by poisoned broth. He was killed three weeks into the marriage.

It was at this stage though that the activities of Elizabeth Ridgeway attracted suspicion. Apprentices of Thomas Ridgeway recalled that he had complained of his broth being gritty and strange when he ate his fateful doom laden meal (which had occurred in a church of all places). The apprentices noticed that when Elizabeth served them some porridge soon after it also had a gritty texture. They were too suspicious to eat any of it and deduced what was happening. Elizabeth was trying to kill them to secure their silence. Once Elizabeth realised they were onto her she tried to bribe them in return for silence but they reported her to Thomas Ridgeway's relatives.

A medical examination of the body of Thomas Ridgeway confirmed that he had been poisoned. Cruentation was used to test Elizabeth's guilt. What is cruentention? According to definitions.net - 'Cruentation (Latin: "ius cruentationis" or "Ius feretri sine sandapilae") was one of the medieval methods of finding proof against a suspected murderer. The common belief was that the body of the victim would spontaneously bleed in the presence of the murderer.' Elizabeth Ridgeway was found guilty and sentenced to death. As this was 1684, the method was execution was death by burning at the stake! There were some attempts to reduce her sentence and show a little more mercy (burning at the stake is pretty extreme) but it was the refusal of Elizabeth to offer confessions to a local clergyman that sealed her fate. She had no interest in begging God for forgiveness.

(91) MARY BELL (Years Active 1968, Two Victims)

Mary Flora Bell was born in Newcastle, England, in 1957. Mary Bell is often cited as one of the youngest serial killers. She was ten when she strangled two toddlers in Newcastle in 1968. It is debatable that two murders made Mary Bell a serial killer but most experts believe she would almost certainly have killed again if she hadn't been caught. Mary Bell had some of the traits we associate with serial killers. She seemed to enjoy the attention the murders brought to her area and even left a cryptic (if childish) confession note in a local nursery. Mary, who was manipulative and intelligent, also tried to pin the deaths on her best friend Norma.

Mary Bell, by any standards, had an awful childhood. Her mother Betty Bell was an alcoholic prostitute who tried to give Mary away on several occasions. Betty Bell could be violent and was subject to unpredictable mood swings. There were beatings in addition to verbal assaults on Mary Bell and her siblings. All of this clearly took its toll on Mary Bell in particular. Mary Bell also endured several drug overdoses as a child thanks to the pills her mother would both give her and absently leave around the house.

Decades after the terrible events of 1968, Mary Bell would claim that she had been sexually abused as a child by the men that her mother brought back to the house as a prostitute. Mary Bell would blame her mother for the creation of the 'demon child' she had been in 1968. It is speculated that the overdoses Mary was subject to may have left her with some form of brain damage that was never diagnosed.

Mary was clearly an odd child from a very young age. She never cried or showed much sign of emotion. Perhaps the key incident in Mary's early life came when she was five years-old and witnessed another child be killed by a bus. Mary seemed to suffer from a form of PTSD after this incident. She found it difficult to bond with other children or make friends. Mary's first kindergarten teacher said she was a nightmare. Mary would pinch, hit, and throttle the other children and she was constantly making up tall stories. Despite her often nightmarish family life, Mary Bell was a surprisingly bright and intelligent child though. She was smart and streetwise and had an aptitude for writing and poetry. Even at a tender age, Mary Bell had a quick deadpan wit and inquisitive mind.

Mary had also grown into a pretty girl. She had an oval face, a bob haircut with a long black fringe, and piercing blue eyes. Her ethereal blue eyes spooked and unsettled the other children at Delaval Road Junior School whenever she gazed at them. A frequent description of Mary at this time from those who encountered her was that she seemed completely unemotional. Mary seemed like a tabula rasa. When she stared at the other children they had a troubling sense that someone very cold and indifferent had fixed their steely gaze upon them.

Two doors down from Mary Bell on Whitehouse Road lived a girl named Norma Joyce Bell (who was not related to Mary despite sharing a surname). The pair became friends and would always spend much time in one another's company. Mary and Norma would become inextricably linked in the Mary Bell story. Norma was two years older than Mary but had a low IQ. She was easily dominated by Mary and very much what you might call the junior sidekick in their friendship - despite being older and taller.

Mary Bell was constantly in trouble with the police. She was spoken to for pushing a little boy off a ledge. Around the same time, a mother complained that Mary Bell had tried to strangle her seven year-old daughter Pauline Watson in a children's sandpit at the local nursery. Mary had stuffed sand in the girl's mouth as she throttled her. Mary Bell was disruptive and a bully. She was clearly dangerous.

The Tyneside area where Mary lived was undergoing a massive social change in the 1960s. Urban slum housing at this time had to be demolished to make way for more modern accommodation. This demolition was on a grand scale. Whole streets were being torn down brick by brick. So the area where Mary Bell roamed as a child became littered with derelict houses and cement strewn wasteland as this huge urban regeneration process was undertaken. Children would play in the rubble and tentatively explore the strange abandoned houses. This was their urban playground.

On the 25th of May, 1968, a four year-old boy named Martin Brown was playing outside with his friends. Martin strayed into the area known as Rat Alley. He was curly haired and described as a cheeky and energetic child by his family. Tragically, this would be the last day of Martin's short life. Martin was found upstairs on the floor in a derelict house by three children at 3:30 p.m. on Saturday afternoon. He was dribbling saliva from his mouth and looked inert. Mary Bell had killed him by squeezing his neck.

Before Martin had been taken away to hospital, children had started to gather at the derelict house where he was found to see what all the drama was about. Amongst the first to arrive were Mary Bell and Norma. Mary was eager to push her way in and get a clear view. She seemed intent on showing Norma this tragic scene in the flesh. The children were all ushered away by the workmen and told to go home. It was only in retrospect that Mary's uncanny ability to get to the scene of these tragedies became suspicious.

What was even more suspicious at the time was Mary's apparent excitement at these terrible crime scenes and resulting local investigations. Mary and Norma used to sometimes babysit for Rita Finlay - the sister of Martin Brown's mother June. Mary now rushed around to the home of Martin Brown's aunt to tell her that something had happened to Martin. Mary's interactions with this family would come to be seen as cruel and perverse.

Dr Bernard Knight was the pathologist who had to examine Martin's body for the official police report. Dr Knight found that there were no conclusive indicators which showed how the boy had died. Martin hadn't taken any tablets and there were no obvious signs of severe violence against the child - although a minor head injury was apparent. The conclusion of the autopsy was that the death was most likely a tragic accident. The next day came a most curious incident. The police were called when the Day Nursery on Woodlands Crescent at the end of Whitehouse Road was broken into. What the police found at the scene was very shocking and rather strange. They found four notes - written in a child's scrawl with spelling mistakes - apparently confessing to the murder of Martin Brown. The notes had been written by May and Norma - who had smuggled themselves in through a loose slate on the roof.

On the 31st of July, three year-old Brian Howe was watching the demolition of houses in Rat Alley. He was never seen alive again. Brian was Mary's second victim. Mary even told Brian's sister Pat where she'd last seen him playing. A patch of wasteground known as the Tin Lizzie. A place of cement blocks and oil drums. This was where Brian was later found dead. Mary had clearly been trying to direct Pat to the area where the body was. She obviously wanted to see Pat's reaction when she discovered Brian. It was yet another callous addition to the already disturbing story of Mary Bell.

Brian Howe was found by the police just after 11 pm. He was lying dead between two concrete blocks. Some of his hair had been snipped off and there were puncture wounds on his legs and some mutilation of his genitals. There were pressure marks on his nose. The cuts to his legs were caused after death. A pair of bent scissors was found near the scene. When the pathologist determined that the death was most likely caused by a child, the police re-opened the Martin Brown case - given its obvious similarities to this fresh tragedy. The police now strongly suspected that Martin had been murdered too. "If she hadn't murdered Brian," said June Richardson, the mother of Martin Brown, "she would have committed the perfect crime. Everyone thought Martin had died from natural causes but after that, the police put two and two together."

Mary Bell and Norma Bell were brought to trial for the murder of Martin Brown and Brian Howe at the Newcastle Assizes Moot Hall on December the 5th 1968. Norma was completely innocent but Mary had dragged her friend in this awful affair. Mary Bell - famously - seemed to show little visible sign of emotion for much of the trial. Rather as she had done during her interviews with the police, Mary came across as a shrewd and tough little girl to those in court. She had a quick answer for most of questions put to her and seemed remarkably poised and in control for one so young. The tearful Norma, by contrast, seemed overwhelmed by the whole experience.

The jury only took four hours to return a verdict. Mary was found guilty of manslaughter on diminished grounds. Norma was acquitted of all charges on the grounds that she was of low intelligence and had been dominated by her friend. Mary was - rightly - deemed the child who had killed the boys. She was sentenced to be detained at Her Majesty's pleasure - effectively an indefinite sentence of imprisonment.

Mary Bell was shuttled around various approved schools and young offenders institutions before a stint in prison in her late teens. In 1980, while in her early twenties, she was released and given a new identity. Mary Bell later got married and had a child. Today she is a grandmother. Mary Bell is proof that rehabilitation (especially at a young age) can work but nothing will ever erase the sadness that came with the loss of two children in 1968. The dark legend of Mary Bell has never completely faded away. It probably never will.

(90) DOROTHY WILLIAMS (Years Active 1987-1989, Three Victims)

Dorothy Williams was born in 1954. She was responsible for three murders in Cook County, Illinois, which took place between 1987 and 1989. Williams was a thief who lived a

rough sort of street life where crime and violence was rife.
Even before her most awful crimes, she was not unknown to
the police and had three convictions in the 1970s for drugs
possession and assault (including one on a police officer). The
motivation for her three murders was money to fund her drug
habit. Dorothy Williams was a heroin addict and her desperate
desire to get money to buy drugs made her a very dangerous
woman who was perfectly willing to resort to murder.

Williams targeted senior citizens' housing projects in the area.
She would adopt various ruses as a means to get access to the
vulnerable and elderly. Sometimes she would pretend to be a
care worker. It is said that she would sometimes also simply
knock on someone's door and ask for a glass of water. Seventy-
nine-year-old Lonnie Laws was the first victim of Williams. He
was strangled by a belt. Dorothy Williams was a large and
powerful woman and an elderly and frail person would have
stood little chance of fighting her off - especially if caught by
surprise.

In 1988, Williams stabbed to death 63 year-old Cesar Zuell.
Zuell suffered three fatal stab wounds to the chest in the
violent attack. The final murder by Williams was the most
callous of all. She strangled 97-year-old Mary Harris with a
scarf. These brutal murders only netted Williams about $50
from each victim and a modest stereo (which she stole from
the home of her last victim). It was a pathetic amount of
money to kill three people over and an illustration of how
ruthless and evil Dorothy Williams was. It was later
established that Williams had also robbed four other residents
in the senior citizens' housing project.

Thankfully, Dorothy Williams was not the most difficult
person to catch. She'd left fingerprints all over the scene of her
heartless crimes and other residents had seen her in the
building and were able to give a description of the suspect to
the police. The prosecution wanted the death penalty for
Williams and they got their wish at the 1991 trial when she was
sentenced to die by lethal injection. However, Illinois governor

George Ryan downsized her sentence to life with parole in 2003. Prosecutor John McNerney described Dorothy Williams at the trial as "a reverse Robin Hood who steals from those who have nothing and uses it for her own selfish interests." Dorothy Williams is now serving three life sentences behind bars and this is where she will remain for the rest of her days.

(89) FAYE COPELAND (Years Active 1986-1989, 5+ Victims)

Ray and Faye Copeland are - at 76 and 69 - the oldest couple to be sentenced to death in the United States. They conspired to murder five farm workers on their farm in Mooresville, Missouri between 1986 and 1989. Ray Copeland used the farm workers (who were mostly drifters looking for some temporary work) to buy cattle with dodgy cheques and then shot the workers so that nothing could be traced back to him. Fay was judged to be in on their murderous scheme.

Faye was born in 1921. Her husband Ray had a string of past convictions for petty frauds and thefts but there was nothing that indicated he was capable of murder. Until that is a number of men started to go missing after picking up a ride with Ray. In 1989 the police received an anonymous telephone call from a man who claimed to have found human bones on the farm belonging to Ray and Faye Copeland. Locals always found Ray a rather choleric and strange character. He - rather suspiciously in hindsight - was often seen stopping to talk to drifters and vagrants.

The police deduced that workers for Ray had been used to buy cattle with bogus funds and had then mysteriously disappeared. When he was spoken to, Ray denied knowing anything about the men or the bad cheques. A likely story indeed. Of course he knew. When the police searched the farm they found three bodies buried near a barn. The victims had been shot in the back of the head. It is not known how many victims there were on this farm of horror. Most people think the Copeland's killed more than five people.

As is often the case with women who are an accomplice to a male killer, Faye tried to pretend she was a victim herself. She said she was abused by her husband and had no idea that he'd been killing people. This risible defence was blown apart though when the police found notes and diaries written by Faye Copeland in which she'd written down and logged the names of the victims. She was no innocent bystander at all. The Copelands were charged with five counts of first-degree murder. Faye went up first in 1990 and was sentenced to death. "These things happen," Ray Copeland is to have calmly remarked when he learned of Faye's sentence. Obviously not a man prone to too much emotion was Ray Copeland!

The following year Ray Copeland also received the death penalty. Neither Ray or Faye Copeland were executed in the end though. Ray Copeland died in prison in 1993 and Faye Copeland, who had her sentence commuted to life in prison, died in 2002. Faye Copeland died in a nursing home after Governor Bob Holden agreed to a request for a medical parole. Ray and Faye Copeland were a pretty deadly couple by any standards. They were both perfectly happy to have five (and possibly more) murders on their conscience simply for a little financial gain. This unlikely serial killer duo would clearly have been responsible for many more deaths if they hadn't been caught in 1989.

(88) SHEILA LABARRE (Years Active 2004-2006, Two Verified Victims, Other Suspected Victims)

Sheila LaBarre was born Sheila Kaye Bailey in Alabama in 1958. She got married in the 1970s but she was always a rather troubled woman and spent some time in a psychiatric facility in 1980 after a suicide attempt. In 1981 she got married again but this union was obviously not very long lasting or harmonious because in 1987 she moved in with a chiropractor named Bill LaBarre (from whom she took her last name - despite there being no evidence that they were ever legally married).

Sheila LaBarre did get married though in 1995 to a man named Wayne Ennis. This marriage only lasted about a year and a half. Sheila LaBarre said that Ennis was abusive and she eventually filed a restraining order so that he couldn't come anywhere near her. After the death of Bill LaBarre, Sheila LaBarre claimed to be his common law wife and inherited his farm as a consequence. You can imagine how Bill LaBarre's children from his previous marriages felt about this. They were not happy at all but declined to contest the inheritance in the end because it would have them cost a tidy sum of money in legal fees and have no guarantee of success.

Sheila LaBarre was now alone on the farm and it soon transpired that her mental health was fragile to say the least. In 2006 she made contact with a 24 year-old man named Kenny Countie through a personal advert. Countie had learning difficulties and was said to be a rather childlike man who was easily manipulated. Sheila LaBarre, who was clearly not the full shilling, accused Countie of being a paedophile and stabbed him to death. She then burned the body in an attempt to mask the murder.

Sheila LaBarre supposedly lived at the farm by this time with a man named Michael Deloge. However, no one had seen Deloge since 2005. There was a good reason for this. Sheila LaBarre had killed him. A bone belonging to Deloge and a spent shell casing was found at the farm in 2008. The precise circumstances of Deloge's death remain a mystery. Michael Deloge's mother kicked up a fuss about his disappearance and claimed that Sheila LaBarre had always wanted to kill him. It was a good job that Deloge's mother did speak up because everything she accused Sheila LaBarre of was true.

The police decided to go and search the farm and the plot

thickened when they found human toes that (it eventually transpired through DNA tests) did not belong to either Deloge or Kenny Countie. Remains and DNA also confirmed that Delogue and Countie had been killed on the farm. Sheila LaBarre (who pleaded not guilty by reasons of insanity) was sentenced to life in prison without parole in June 2008. How many people Sheila LaBarre actually killed remains unclear. The human toes obviously indicate there was at least one more victim. The death of Bill LaBarre is also retrospectively seen as rather suspicious. One thing is clear though. Sheila LaBarre was a very dangerous and ruthless woman and her farm was the last place you'd want to visit.

(87) LEONARDA CIANCIULLI (Years Active 1939-1940, Three Victims)

Leonarda Cianciulli was born in Montella, Avellino, in 1894. Leonarda Cianciulli was a serial killer active in Italy during World War 2. Her murders were unusual because they were motivated by a belief in black magic. Cianciulli believed that if she offered up some human sacrifices this would prevent her soldier son from coming to any harm in the war. She subsequently killed three women. The story of Leonarda Cianciulli was given a macabre gloss by what she did to her victims after she killed them. She used the blood from her victims in a recipe for tea cakes. Cianciulli also turned her last victim into bars of soap. And yes, Leonarda Cianciulli is said to have sampled the cakes she made from her unfortunate victims.

Her first victim was a spinster named Faustina Sett who had come to Cianciulli for advice in matters of the heart. She wanted Cianciulli to help her find a husband. Cianciulli told Sett she knew of a man but Sett would have to travel to meet him. Cianciulli told Sett to write postcards and post them when she got there. She then drugged Sett with tainted wine and chopped the body up, keeping the blood in a basin. Cianciulli then made cakes out of the blood.

Of her victim blood cakes, Leonarda Cianciulli said - "I threw the pieces into a pot, added seven kilos of caustic soda, which I had bought to make soap, and stirred the mixture until the pieces dissolved in a thick, dark mush that I poured into several buckets and emptied in a nearby septic tank. As for the blood in the basin, I waited until it had coagulated, dried it in the oven, ground it and mixed it with flour, sugar, chocolate, milk and eggs, as well as a bit of margarine, kneading all the ingredients together. I made lots of crunchy tea cakes and served them to the ladies who came to visit, though Giuseppe and I also ate them."

Cianciulli's next victim was Francesca Soav, a woman who required help finding a job. Cianciulli said she had found a suitable position somewhere but then - as before - drugged the victim and made cakes from the dead body after boiling down the other remains. Although these sacrifices were supposed to be some sort of 'dark magic' offerings for the safety of her son, money was an equal motivation. Cianciulli had obtained money from both victims for her services.

The last victim was Virginia Cacioppo. Virginia Cacioppo was a soprano who Cianciulli claimed to have found a secretarial position for. This victim was not just made into cakes but also soap. "She ended up in the pot, like the other two...her flesh was fat and white, when it had melted I added a bottle of cologne, and after a long time on the boil I was able to make some most acceptable creamy soap. I gave bars to neighbours and acquaintances. The cakes, too, were better: that woman was really sweet." Cianciulli said she almost decapitated Virginia Cacioppo by striking her with an axe.

Cianciulli was given a long prison sentence and died in a criminal asylum in 1970. She was 76 years-old. Cianciulli had a troubled time as a young woman as her parents didn't approve of her marriage. She also lost several to her children to miscarriages or illness. This sad experience left her a very superstitious woman who believed in fortune tellers and the occult. This strong belief in the occult is the only real explanation one can put forward as a reason for her bizarre crimes.

(86) CAROLE M. BUNDY (Years Active 1980, Two Victims)

The Sunset Strip Killers were Doug Clark and Carol M. Bundy. This was a rather bizarre couple that had sick fantasies. Clark is believed to have killed six people (mostly young girls and teenagers) and Bundy would assist in luring the victims. She procured him guns and then lured underage girls for him. The necrophiliac Doug Clark was a very evil and disturbing man. Bundy killed alone too when she shot and decapitated a former lover she was in a dispute with. She was convicted of two murders in the end.

Carol M. Bundy was born in 1942. Both of her parents were alcoholics. She claimed her father molested her and she ended up in various foster homes. Bundy ended up getting married three times and had two children with her last husband (who was said to be abusive and not exactly husband of the year material). Carol famously also had a (sarcasm intended) Richard Burton/Elizabeth Taylor style romance with her apartment manager Jack Murray. Jack wanted to be a country singer and Carol was so smitten she even tried to bribe Jack's wife to let him leave his marriage.

Carol was 37 when she came under the shadow of the awful Doug Clark. She was pretty awful and evil herself too and help facilitate his murders and obsession with dark sexual fantasies that involved young girls. When Doug killed one victim and brought home a severed head, Carol put make-up on the head and allowed him to sexually abuse it. In 1980, Carol became worried that Jack Murray, who she still saw and confided in, might tell the cops about Doug Clark. So she lured Murray to his van and shot him. She then decapitated Murray after the murder. Why did she remove the head? It was apparently so she wouldn't leave ballistic evidence. Doug Clark helped her dispose of the head in a trash can.

Despite her concern over ballistic evidence, Carol M. Bundy was clearly no H.H Holmes when it came to covering her tracks. She had been seen with Murray earlier and also left some shell casings in his van. Bundy now decided to phone the cops and report Doug Clark in the vague (and ultimately doomed) hope that it might make her seem less suspicious. Bundy soon buckled under pressure though and confessed to everything she had done - both alone and with Clark. Doug Clark claimed that Bundy shot one of the female victims he raped so she is generally credited with two 'solo' murders. The murder of Jack Murray alone though was enough to give Carol M. Bundy some sort of place in any list of the deadliest female killers.

Doug Clark, in the tragi-comic and incompetent tradition of Rodney Alcala and Ted Bundy, defended himself at his trial and tried to claim that Carol M. Bundy had done all the murders alone. You can imagine how that went for him. That's right. Doug Clark ended up on death row (where he still resides today). Carol M. Bundy tried to plead insanity at first but then reversed this and offered a confession. In her first confession she told the police that the murders were 'fun' and that she'd do it all again given the chance. In the end it was only a plea deal that spared her from a death sentence.

Carol M. Bundy was sentenced to a prison term of 25 years for Murray's murder and a term of 27 years for the second murder. She died in prison in 2003 at the age of 61. By any standards she was a seriously strange and dangerous woman. Many crime experts think that Bundy and Clark were almost certainly responsible for a lot more murders than we are yet aware of. Carol M. Bundy is sometimes compared to the British killer Rose West in that she was a murderous accomplice to a very twisted and weird man. Bundy and West also looked rather similar too as both had dark hair and wore very large spectacles.

(85) MARTHA RENDELL (Years Active 1907-1908, Three Murders)

Martha Rendell was born in 1871 in Australia. This was an awful woman by any standards who responsible for terrible crimes that begger belief. Rendell was the common-law wife of a man named Thomas Morris and murdered his three young children. The method in which she did this was exceptionally cruel. Rendell swabbed their throats with spirits of salts (hydrochloric acid). This caused inflammation and haemorrhage of the bowel. The throats of the children became inflamed to the point where they could no longer eat. They all died agonising and slow deaths.

Seven year-old Annie was the first victim and then Rendell did the same to Olive (aged five) and Arthur (aged fourteen). The family doctor though could find no evidence of anything suspicious about the deaths at first. This was clearly incompetence on his part. Martha Rendell's wicked and unfathomable crimes only came to light when she tried to do the same to the remaining son George. George got suspicious though and ran away. The police got involved in a search for George and when they found him the boy told them that Rendell had killed his siblings and was now trying to poison him with spirits of salts.

Exhumations of George's siblings took place and foul play was (not before time you might suggest) finally discovered. Diluted hydrochloric acid was found to be present in the throat tissue of the dead children. Martha Rendell pretended to be innocent and claimed a doctor had prescribed spirits of salts for the children but her defence was flimsy to say the least. Thomas Morris was actually charged with the murders too but he was acquitted in the end. These dreadful crimes had been the work of Martha Rendell alone.

As you can imagine, there was a lot of public anger in Australia when these hideous crimes came to light. The public would happily have lynched Martha Rendell given half a chance. There was never much danger of her getting anything but the sternest sentence possible. Rendell was hanged in Fremantle Prison on October the 6th, 1909. She was the last woman to be hanged in Western Australia. Her motivation for murder is presumed to have been the fact that she didn't like the children very much and resented having to share her husband's time and attention with them. So she simply decided to kill them in an exceptionally cruel way.

Before her execution, she declared 'I most solemnly wish to state that on this, the last morning of my life. I am innocent before God and man of having done anything that injured the children in any degree. The spirits of salts were never used by me on the children. If I had done it, I would confess. I believe it would be contrary to my most solemn convictions to profess to man to be innocent when before God I should be found guilty, which would be to me dying with a lie on my lips and a crime on my soul unconfessed — unforgiven. I pray to God to give me grace to forgive those who have sworn falsely my life away.' As that statement suggests, Martha Rendell never showed any remorse for her crimes. Despite the overwhelming evidence she went to the gallows still pretending to be innocent.

(84) LYDA SOUTHARD (Years Active 1915–1920, Six Victims)

Lyda Southard was born in Keytesville, Missouri in 1892. She had six husbands in all and killed four of them. As if that wasn't bad enough she also killed her daughter and brother in law. You probably won't be surprised to learn that Lyda is commonly known as The Black Widow in true crime circles. Her first husband was Robert C. Dooley. The couple had a daughter together named Lorraine. Tragedy seemed to quickly surround Lyda though. Her daughter, husband, and her husband's brother all died in fairly quick succession.

Lyda explained away the death of her daughter by saying the child had drunk water from a polluted well. That was a blatant lie but it seemed to fool everyone at the time. Her husband's death was judged to have been from ptomaine poisoning and her brother in law was presumed to have been a victim of typhoid. Because people often died a lot younger in this era than they do today and medical science was far less sophisticated, poisoners like Lyda Southard were able to get away their crimes for longer than you'd imagine. If someone suddenly dropped dead of mysteriously fell ill in the early part of the 20th century it wasn't necessarily deemed to be suspicious.

A year or so later, Lyda married a man named William G. McHaffle but he died not very long into the marriage at all. In 1919 she married another man - this time Harlan Lewis. Within short three months of the couple getting hitched, Harlan Lewis was dead. Lyda then moved to Idaho and married a man named Edward Meyer. This marriage lasted a grand total of one month before Meyer dropped dead! As you might expect and hope, Lyda had by now finally started to attract suspicion concerning her remarkably bad misfortune when it came to husbands and relatives dropping dead all over the place.

An investigation into Edward Meyer's death established that arsenic had been responsible for his swift demise. Remarkably, while the authorities were trying to find Lyda Southard, she actually got married again. This was to Paul Southard (from whom she got her most commonly used name). Lyda tried to persuade Paul Southard to take out life insurance but he refused because he was in the army and already had this covered. At this point, Lyda was finally captured and given a ten-years-to-life sentence in the Old Idaho State Penitentiary.

Incredibly, Lyda Southard escaped from prison in 1931 and actually got married again while on the run! When she apprehended, Lyda served another eleven years in prison before earning parole. She died of a heart attack in 1958 in Salt Lake City, Utah. Lyda Southard was 65 at the time of her death. She is generally credited with six victims but it seems safe to assume that Lyda probably tried (and certainly planned) to kill a lot more people than that.

(83) KIMBERLY CLARK SAENZ (Years Active 2008, Five Victims)

Kimberly Clark Saenz was born in Fall River, Massachusetts in 1973. Saenz was another of those awful medical killers. She used her position as a nurse to murder patients. Saenz killed five patients and is believed to have attempted to murder five more. Although she was married with two children, Saenz was a troubled woman who was hooked on prescription drugs and had a conviction for public intoxication. Saenz had a battery of nursing jobs in her life but was fired more than once. She was dismissed from one hospital for stealing Demerol and then trying to fake the drug test she was subsequently obliged to take.

Saenz ended up at DaVita's Lufkin clinic in Texas - which dealt with patients on dialysis. A strangely high number of patients at the clinic began to suffer from cardiac problems after Saenz began working there. Paramedics were bewildered and very concerned by this sudden spike in cardiac incidents and asked the hospital to launch an investigation. DaVita consequently sent some surveyors to the clinic to see if they could find out what the problem was. The investigation established that Kimberly Clark Saenz had been on shift for 85% of the cardiac emergencies. This was clearly highly suspicious and probably not a coincidence.

Two patients then gave statements in which they claimed they had seen Saenz injecting other patients with sodium hypochlorite. Sodium hypochlorite is better known as bleach. The clinic was closed after syringes used by Saenz showed clear traces of bleach. It was then established that in google searches on the personal computer of Saenz she had researched if bleach could kill someone if it was injected. Other nurses also gave accounts of how Saenz would talk about which patients she didn't like and show no remorse when they went into cardiac arrest or died.

Although this all sounds like an open and shut case it wasn't quite that simple in the end. There was relatively little scientific research in detecting bleach in the blood so they had to get in scientific experts to build a case. These experts had to prove and explain how an agent like bleach would produce a reaction in the body that could result in cardiac arrest. They thankfully managed to do this in the end. Prosecutors wanted the death penalty for Saenz but at her 2012 trial she received life in prison. Kimberly Clark Saenz appealed her conviction in 2015 but to no avail. The evidence against her at the trial was simply too overwhelming and conclusive.

(82) MARY JANE JACKSON (Years Active 1856-1861, Four Victims)

Mary Jane Jackson was born in 1836 on Gridon Street and was a New Orleans prostitute. You might say that Jackson was sort like an early version of Aileen Wuornos in that she was a sex worker (so often the targets for serial killers) but a killer rather than a victim. Jackson flipped this familiar serial killer trope upside down. Mary Jane Jackson was known as Bricktop because of her red hair. She became a prostitute at the age of thirteen but she had a fierce temper and was more than handy with her fists.

In 1856, Mary Jane Jackson beat a man to death with a club in the French Quarter. The motivation for the murder was that he had called Mary a whore. The next victim of Mary Jane Jackson was a man named Long Charley. This was an exceptionally tall and strong man but Mary killed him by use of a lethal dagger she always carried around for personal protection. Mary opened her own brothel in the end and in

1859 stabbed to death a man named Laurent Fleury in a tavern after he commented that women couldn't hold their drink.

Amazingly, Mary was not charged with Laurent Fleury's murder because the coroner could not establish a cause of death - despite several stab wounds! It is naturally assumed then that Mary must have given this coroner money in return for getting her off the hook. Mary then met a young man named John Miller. Miller worked as a manager in the world of boxing. The relationship between Mary and John Miller was obstreperous and rowdy to say the least.

Mary and John Miller were constantly fighting and this wasn't just verbal jousting. They would literally punch each other and get into real fights. They always seemed to patch things up and get back together though. However, in 1861 they get into another violent fight when Miller attempted to give Mary a thrashing. Trying to give Mary Jane Jackson a thrashing was about as sensible as sticking your head in the mouth of a T-Rex.

What made this fight even more bizarre is that Miller had a missing arm and had replaced the limb with a ball and chain! He was like some medieval knight. Miller suddenly brandished a knife in the scuffle but Mary managed to get hold of it and then stabbed him to death. She was sentenced to ten years in prison for the murder but several months later the newly appointed Union Army governor of New Orleans issued blanket pardons for prisoners. Mary Jane Jackson was free and what happened to her afterwards remains a mystery. She kept a low profile after her unexpected release and was never heard from again.

(81) THE LETHAL LOVERS (Years Active 1987, Five Verified Victims)

Gwendolyn Graham (born 1963) and Cathy Wood (born 1962) became known as The Lethal Lovers after killing five patients in Michigan's Alpine Manor. This diabolical duo were nursing aides and lovers. The victims were - Mae Mason, 79, Edith Cole, 89, Marguerite Chambers, 60, Myrtle Luce, 95, and Belle Burkhard, 74. Graham and Wood first met in 1986 and moved in together. They killed their first victim at the start of 1987 and got away with it because the death was deemed to have been as a result of natural causes.

Graham and Wood wanted to choose victims whose names spelled out MURDER as part of a sick private game but they abandoned this plan in the end because it proved too difficult. The patients were suffocated by the duo. They believed that by killing together they would cement an unbreakable bond. The murderous duo eventually went their separate ways though and this split led to their downfall. That unbreakable bond obviously wasn't as unbreakable as they thought. Gwendolyn Graham began a relationship with another nurse and then moved to Texas.

The crimes of Wood and Graham came to light because of Wood's ex-husband. Cathy Wood had confessed the murders to him and he went to the police. When the police interviewed Wood she confessed to the murders and said they suffocated the patients with washcloths. Wood testified against Graham at the trial and as a consequence Graham was convicted of first-degree murder of all five victims and handed five life sentences. Wood received a sentence based on her guilty plea of one charge of conspiracy to commit murder and one charge of second-degree murder.

Cathy Wood was granted parole by the Michigan Department of Corrections in 2018 and in 2020 she was released. The relatives of the victims were very upset by this and believe that Wood downplayed her own role in the murders to get a lesser charge than Gwendolyn Graham. Some retrospectives of this case have argued that Wood was the most dangerous of the duo and the brains and driving force behind the whole murderous operation. Gwendolyn Graham, in a prison interview, said that Cathy wood was 'evil' and expressed astonishment that her partner in crime was now a free woman.

Retired police officer Roger Kaliniak, who was involved in the case when the two women were investigated and arrested, said he was rather surprised to learn that Cathy Wood had been released. "She's a serial killer and she could do it again, and most of them do," he said. "I believe that Cathy Wood was the mastermind, she was the one that was pulling strings on Gwendolyn Graham. Gwendolyn Graham handled the dirty work and Cathy Wood was the brains behind it. "

Court documents from the trial suggested that the two women tried to kill at least ten patients in all. The only crumb of comfort from this awful case is that the two women went their separate ways fairly quickly. The body count would have been considerably higher if they hadn't. Graham and Woods were later the inspiration for a 2016 episode of American Horror Story where two nurses named Miranda and Bridget decide to kill their patients.

(80) MARIANNE NOLLE (Years Active 1984-1992, 7+ Victims)

Marianne Nölle was born in 1938 in Cologne, North Rhine-Westphalia, Germany. Nölle is another in the long line of medical killers. To the world at large she was a competent and respected nurse but in reality she was killed patients with overdoses of Truxal. Chlorprothixene, sold under the brand name Truxal, is a sedative and antipsychotic. Overdose symptoms can be confusion, hypertension, and tachycardia. Nölle killed seven patients from 1984 to 1992 but she is believed to have attempted to kill around seventeen patients in all.

The oldest victim of Marianne Nölle was 91 years-old. None of the victims were terminally ill. Marianne Nölle would rob the victims after she killed them and take any money or valuables they had with them. Her heartless crimes eventually began to attract suspicion. A grandson of one of her victims started to become suspicious and scrutiny of Marianne Nölle became heightened as a consequence. With more relatives and also a hospital supervisor becoming suspicious, exhumations took place which established that Nölle's patients had not died of natural causes at all. They had been hastened to their grave by this wicked medical killer.

Marianne Nölle was 57 years-old by the time of her trial. She sat silent through most of it and only spoke at the end to insist she was innocent. In 1993 she was sentenced to life in prison. Nölle, in a rare show of emotion, became tearful at this. The judge described Marianne Nölle as a very heartless and manipulative two faced woman. Her patients all loved her but little did they know she was only interested in killing them so that she could take what little money or valuables they might have.

Marianne Nölle never confessed to any of her crimes or provided any explanation for why she had killed these patients. The judge at the trial she she had taken it upon herself to play 'master' over life and death. Her guilt was never in question as four cans of Truxal were found in her apartment after she was arrested. The chilling thing about Marianne Nölle is that her patients all trusted her because she seemed so genuine and caring. Little did they know how dangerous she really was.

(79) LUDIVINE CHAMBERT (Years Active 2012–2013, Ten Victims)

Ludivine Chambet was born in France in 1983. Chambet worked in a number of nursing homes around Jacob-Bellecombette in Savoie and was the employed at Chambéry hospital. Chambet had a form of gigantism which gave her a very oversized body and some deformations. As a result of this she suffered from ridicule at school - which must have left mental scars. She was later an unlicensed nursing assistant and seemed like a perfectly kind and caring woman to those that knew her.

It is speculated that Chamet's mental health began to erode after the death of her mother in 2013. Chambet was exceptionally close to her mother and felt lost and adrift in the world after her mother passed away. Chambet had no friends or love life and her world revolved around her mother. After her mother passed away, she suffered from a deep depression and - eventually - began to do some unexplainable and tragic things.

Chambet began killing patients in the nursing home l'Ehpad du Césalet at Chambéry she worked in by giving them large quantities of drugs like neuroleptics and antidepressants. These patients, many of whom were elderly, feel into comas from which they never recovered. The patients killed by Chambet were not terminal and would have got better were it not for Chambet murdering them. What rumbled Chambet was the death of an 83 year-old woman who had Parkinsons. The nursing home had experienced a number of patient deaths which seemed somewhat mysterious and they soon deduced that the common factor was Ludivine Chambet. Chambet had been on duty for all of these slightly strange patient deaths.

In 2013, Chambet was arrested. She confessed to killing a number of patients but said she had done so to alleviate their suffering. This defence is one that all medical serial killers seem to use and in Chambet's case, as with most others, it simply didn't wash. What had really killed these patients it seems was Chambet's descent into mental illness. In 2017 Ludivine Chambet was found guilty of ten homicides and sentenced to 25 years in prison.

Chambet's treatment by the authorities was humane because of her obvious fragility and mental health problems. It was argued in court that she wasn't really a serial killer because, in her deluded mind, she thought she was helping these patients. However, Chambet did say that she was compelled to kill by a split version of herself she called the 'personality'. A number of serial killers have said something like this after they were captured. Though convicted of ten murders, investigators at the trial believe that Ludivine Chambet probably killed thirteen people. She clearly would have killed a lot more if she hadn't been caught. Ludivine Chambet became known as The Poisoner of Chambéry in the French media.

(78) SACHIKO ETO (Years Active 1994-1995, Six Victims)

Sachiko Eto was born in Japan in 1947. She is known as The Drumstick Killer and her case is strange to say the least. She was apparently married as a young women but in later years got involved in a bogus religious group. Eto set herself up as a guru in Sukagawa City and had a number of followers (which included her daughter). Although she liked to think of herself as a great religious mystic she was essentially a cult leader who espoused meaningless mumbo jumbo. Sachiko Eto claimed to have psychic and supernatural powers but the only superpower she actually possessed was the ability to attract gullible and vulnerable people into her cult.

'Brainwashing,' write Psychology.jrank.org, 'has been used predominantly in reference to severe programs of political indoctrination, although it is used occasionally in connection with certain religious, especially cultic, practices. Brainwashing works primarily by making the victim's existing beliefs and attitudes nonfunctional and replacing them with new ones that will be useful in the environment created by the captor. Basically, the techniques of brainwashing involve the complete removal of personal freedom, independence, and decision-making prerogatives; the radical disruption of existing routine behaviour; the total isolation from, and destruction of loyalties to, former friends and associates; the absolute obedience to authority in all matters; intense physical abuse and threats of injury, death, and permanent imprisonment; and the constant presentation of the new beliefs as the only correct and acceptable alternative to continuing an unenlightened life. These techniques are intended to induce in the victim a state of childlike trust in, and dependency on, the captor.'

Sachiko Eto persuaded her followers that they were infested with demons and that the only way to remove these demons was a beating with taiko sticks (a broad range of Japanese percussion instruments). Eto naturally took the prominent role in these beatings and they were clearly a trifle over the top because six people died as a result. Eto and other followers had literally beaten them to death. Now, one death might be seen as an accident but six? Why didn't Eto stop this ridiculous and deadly practice after the first death?

When a cult member ended up in hospital the local police decided to go and take a look at the home where the cult operated from. They found six decomposing bodies and promptly arrested the 54 year-old Eto in addition to other members of the cult. Eto was sentenced to death and subsequently executed in 2012. "I did it as part of a religious service," said Eto at her trial. "I never thought they were going to die." It's safe to say that this cult was one you really didn't want to be a member of. Not unless you wanted to be beaten to death by Sachiko Eto.

(77) SUZAN CARSON (Years Active 1981-1983, 3+ Victims)

Suzan Carson and Michael Carson were dubbed The San Francisco Witch Killers. They were responsible for three murders from 1981 to 1983. The couple, who were said to take vast quantities of mind-altering drugs, became convinced that it was their mission to kill those in thrall to witchcraft and the occult. They killed a young woman in their apartment by caving her head in with a saucepan, a farm worker (the Carsons had a farm) by strangulation, and a hitchhiker by shooting. When they were apprehended, the Carsons were found to have a hit list of 'evil' people they planned to kill. The list included celebrities like Ronald Reagan and Johnny Carson. Michael Carson, who was absolutely bonkers, said in 1983 that witchcraft, homosexuality, and abortion were all sufficient reasons for the murder of someone.

Michael Bear Carson was born James Carson. He was actually married with a daughter named Jenn but his first wife, correctly deducing that he was becoming increasingly unhinged, fled with their child. The child, Jenn, later recalled - "My mom just saw this person who she loved dearly changing before her eyes. I think she realized he was headed for an explosion. One night we just packed the car and disappeared." Carson changed his name to Michael Bear Carson after hearing voices from God.

Suzan Carson was born Susan Barnes. She was divorced with two sons when she came into the dangerous orbit of James Carson. They were soon inseparable and moved into the Haight-Ashbury neighborhood of San Francisco. The couple had a mystic vision while taking drugs and converted to a form of Islam which they had essentially made up themselves. Keryn Barnes, aged 22 was murdered by the couple in her apartment in San Francisco. She had been stabbed thirteen times. The Carsons later said they killed Keryn because they believed she was an evil witch who practiced black magic.

The Carsons then ran a marijuana farm in Humbult County and their mental health seemed to quickly erode even further during this period. They started to become convinced that the people who visited their farm were witches. Clark Stephens was mutilated and murdered in Humboldt County by the Carsons in 1982. He was shot (supposedly after a dispute with the Carsons) and his body was burned and hidden in some compost. In January 1983, the Carsons were hitchhiking in the Napa Valley in California. Jon Hellyar gave them a ride in his car and some sort of altercation erupted. Suzan stabbed Hellyar in the arm and Michael eventually shot him. This violent episode though had been witnessed by other motorists and the Carsons were fairly swiftly arrested.

The Carsons, bizarrely, then had a press conference in which they confessed to the murders and said they had been doing God's work. Suzan said that the first victim Keryn Barnes had falsely converted to Islam and was draining Suzan of her 'Yogic power' so she had to kill her. Suzan Carson was completely crazy. Michael Carson was equally crazy and said - "Good is created and evil is a like a powerful parasite. It can only copy or feed off of the light."

At the trial the crazy Carsons, despite confessing to the murders at the press conference, pleaded not guilty. In June 1984 they were sentenced to 25 years to life imprisonment for the murder of Karen Barnes. They were later convicted of two more murders (Stephens and Hellyar) and given longer sentences. Suzan Carson and Michael Carson are still suspects in twelve other murders. They both received life in prison for their crimes. Suzan Carson lost her last bid for parole in 2015. She will die behind bars. Jenn Carson, the daughter of Michael Bear Carson, said that her father seemed to change for the worse when he meet Suzan Carson. They were both an awful influence on one another in the end. "It was like a match meeting dynamite," said Jenn Carson of the fateful day that Suzan and Michael met.

(76) MILKA PAVOVIC (Years Active 1934, Six Victims)

Milka Pavlović was born in Kokinac, Kingdom of Croatia-Slavonia in 1905. Pavlović was born into a peasant family and as a young woman got married and worked as a milkmaid (basically someone who milks cows). Her husband was named Rade Pavlović. Milka Pavlović was a miserable looking woman who seemed to have a permanent scowl. She wasn't very popular in the community. In 1934 Pavlović purchased some arsenic for what she claimed was a problem with rats. The recipient of this arsenic was not rats but her husband Rade.

She put the poison in his food and he expired fairly quickly thereafter.

According to Medical News Today - 'The symptoms of arsenic poisoning can be acute, or severe and immediate, or chronic, where damage to health is experienced over a longer period. This will often depend on the method of exposure. A person who has swallowed arsenic may show signs and symptoms within 30 minutes. These may include: drowsiness, headaches, confusion, severe diarrhea. As the arsenic poisoning progresses, the patient may start experiencing convulsions, and their fingernail pigmentation may change. Signs and symptoms associated with more severe cases of arsenic poisoning are: a metallic taste in the mouth and garlicky breath, excess saliva, problems swallowing, blood in the urine, cramping muscles, hair loss, stomach cramps, convulsions, excessive sweating. Arsenic poisoning typically affects the skin, liver, lungs, and kidneys. In the final stage, symptoms include seizures and shock. This could lead to a coma or death.'

Rade's death was not deemed especially suspicious at the time but Milka Pavlović rather pushed her luck thereafter with her rampant arsenic poisoning. She poisoned dozens of relatives and also servants in the house of the family in which she worked. The final straw turned out to be the death of a blacksmith. He had been suddenly taken ill with dreadful stomach pains and died as a result - despite being a healthy and strong man only days before. Locals noted that the death of the blacksmith was suspiciously similar to the sudden and unexpected demise of Rade - the husband of Milka Pavlović.

Milka Pavlović was arrested and eventually confessed that she poisoned all these people for financial gain. Some exhumations took place to establish her guilt. There were six victims (that is to say people who died) of Milka Pavlović in all but it could have been far worse because she attempted to poison dozens of other people who somehow manage to survive and eventually recover. At the trial it transpired that

Pavlović put the arsenic in salt and biscuits. She had even planned to poison a two year-old child to seize an inheritance but (fortunately for the child) this wicked scheme was foiled when Milka Pavlović was arrested. Milka Pavlović was executed by hanging in 1935. She was thirty years-old at the time of her death.

(75) JANIE LOU GIBBS (Years Active 1965-1967, Five Victims)

Janie Lou Gibbs was born in Cordele, Georgia in 1932. The story of Gibbs is rather strange by any standards. She was a mother and wife who had been married for eighteen years and was a highly respected member of local church community. That all changed in the end though. In 1965, Janie Lou Gibbs had a surprising change of career when she became a serial killer poisoner. The first victim was her husband Marvin. She poisoned him and when he was in hospital she brought him in a batch of soup she'd made. Naturally, the soup contained more poison just to finish him off. Marvin's death was not deemed suspicious though and it was assumed by the medical staff that he'd passed away as a result of a liver condition he had.

Several months later, Gibbs killed her youngest son (also named Marvin) by poison. A few months after this she killed another son (who was a teenager) by poisoning him. Strangely, the deaths of her children did not make anyone suspect foul play at the time. Once again it was assumed that medical conditions had resulted in the deaths. It was rather odd though to say the least that Gibbs didn't attract suspicion much earlier. You'd have to be very unlucky to have a husband and two young sons pass away in a matter of months! That's not exactly normal.

What might have mitigated any potential suspicion was the fact that Gibbs donated the life insurance money she was picking up from these family deaths to the church. It wasn't as if she was hoarding up a fortune for herself from these apparent family tragedies. Janie Lou Gibbs now had one teenage son left named Robert. Robert was a young father to a baby named Raymond. Well, you probably don't need to be a master sleuth to guess what happened to Robert and Raymond. Janie Lou Gibbs poisoned both of them. The death of another teenage son and a healthy infant to boot was simply too suspicious to ignore.

The autopsy on Robert found large quantities of arsenic in his system. Exhumations of the husband and other sons of Janie Lou Gibbs also revealed arsenic. She had killed her entire family. It didn't come as a huge surprise that Janie Lou Gibbs was initially deemed unfit to stand trial. She was clearly completely insane. A later trial though gave her life in prison. The police found Gibbs to be a rather bewildering woman when they first arrested her. She rarely answered any questions and mostly just stared off into space in silence. Gibbs never explained why she killed her family. All she said was - "I don't question God's work. The Bible says they will get their reward; and I'm sure they will."

One possible theory for the murders was that Gibbs enjoyed the sympathy and attention she got from neighbours and the church each time she suffered another tragedy. She also enjoyed the fact that she was giving the church money in the form of the life insurance. Her religious beliefs were clearly some sort of factor in the murders but obviously it was the frazzled mental health of Gibbs more than anything that made her unfathomably murder her entire family. She later developed Parkinsons and was treated in humane fashion and released into the care of her sister in 1999. She died in 2010.

(74) TAMARA SAMSONOVA (Years Active 2000–2015, 10+ Suspected Victims)

Tamara Samsonova was born in 1947 in the city of Uzhur. Samsonova tends to be known as The Granny Ripper in true crime circles for reasons that will soon become clear. As a young woman she got married and worked for a travel agency. However her husband mysteriously vanished in 2000. Given what we now know about Tamara Samsonova it doesn't seem like a tremendously outrageous notion to suggest that she might have killed him. Tamara Samsonova was arrested in 2015 after CCTV captured her struggling with various bags which were then found to contain human body parts. The body parts belonged to 79-year-old Valentina Ulanova - who Samsonova was supposed to be caring for.

Samsonova had poisoned the woman and then dismembered her body with a hacksaw. "I came home and put the whole pack of Phenazepamum - 50 pills - into her Olivier salad,' she told the police. 'She liked it very much. I woke up after 2am and she was lying on the floor. So I started cutting her to pieces. It was hard for me to carry her to the bathroom, she was fat and heavy. I did everything at the kitchen where she was lying." Samsonova was also captured in the footage with a saucepan which contained the head of her victim.

The motivation for the murder? Samsonova said she had got fed up with Valentina Ulanova because Valentina had a habit of not washing out the tea cups properly after she'd used them. When the police arrested the 66 year-old Tamara Samsonova they found she had written diaries which featured extensive details on eleven murders she had carried out over the years. It was true too that the local area had had incidences of finding bags of human remains. Samsonova had dumped the headless body of Valentina Ulanova in a street before her arrest.

It was then established that in 2003 Tamara Samsonova had murdered a 44 year-old tenant who was staying with her. His headless and limb free body was also dumped in a street. "I killed my tenant Volodya," she told the police, "cut him to pieces in the bathroom with a knife and put the pieces of his body in plastic bags and threw them away in the different parts of Frunzensky District." The police, on searching the home of Tamara Samsonova, found that she seemed to be obsessed with black magic. This was clearly a nutty and disturbed woman. The Russian media reported that Tamara Samsonova was also a cannibal who claimed to have removed and eaten the lungs of one of her victims.

Tamara Samsonova was sent to a psychiatric treatment hospital while the police began the complicated and difficult task of trying to establish just how many people she did or didn't kill. The answer to that question at this time is anyone's guess. We know that Tamara Samsonova killed at least three people but the true figure could be four times that if her diaries are to be believed.

(73) SHARON ELIZABETH KINNE (Years Active 1960-1964, Three Victims)

Sharon Kinne was born Sharon Elizabeth Hall in 1939. Her story is, by any standards, remarkable and a reminder that occasionally truth really can be stranger than fiction. In 1960 she was a twenty year-old housewife in Independence, Missouri. The police were called to the Kinne house because Sharon's husband James Kinne had died - apparently as a result of an accident involving his own handgun. James had been shot in the head while taking a nap. Sharon told the police that the couple's two year-old daughter had picked up the gun and shot him by accident. A likely story you might think but the police actually believed it. They found Sharon Kinne to be very credible.

Alarm bells probably should have been ringing rather more loudly when Sharon collected $200,000 in life insurance from her husband's death and promptly went out and bought herself a new car. Sharon was having an affair with a married man named Walter Jones at this time but he refused to leave his wife. His wife was a woman named Patricia Jones and Patricia was soon found dead. She had been shot and dumped in a quiet lane. Sharon Kinne even helped join the search for Patricia while Patricia was still officially missing and -

suspiciously - seemed to know where Patricia would be found. She pointed out the body to her lover John Boldisz but told him not to tell the police she was with him when he found the body.

John Boldisz didn't do this though. He told the police that he had found the body of Patricia Jones while with Sharon and the police (who now deduced the link between Sharon and Walter Jones) swiftly arrested Sharon Kinne. There was now too much evidence against her. First we had had the strange death of her husband and now the death of Patricia Jones. At her first trial though, Sharon Kinne was found not guilty of killing Patricia Jones. This is believed to have been because of her ability to charm the all male jury in court. One of the jurors even asked for her autograph after the trial ended.

'Sharon had control of that courtroom,' wrote James Hays. 'She had control of the jury. She had control of the spectators. Everybody's attention was focused on Sharon Kinne, even to the point where on the second day after the trial started, Sharon came moseying in late, fashionably late probably in her mind. The trial went on for about 10 days. The jury came back after deliberating only an hour and a half with a verdict of not guilty. The courtroom erupted in cheers.'

Sharon's charms were not so persuasive in the trial for the murder of James Kinne though. John Boldisz testified against Sharon at this trial and said she always had a desire to see her husband dead. It was also proven at this trial that the couple's two year-old daughter would not have been capable of pulling the trigger of the handgun that killed James. Sharon was sentenced to life in prison but a year later the Missouri Supreme court reversed the murder conviction because of a legal technicality. Two more trials followed and Sharon was released on bail pending the fourth trial.

Sharon then met a Chicago man named Samuel Francis Puglise and went to Mexico City with him. The couple argued though and Sharon then met a man named Francisco Paredes

Ordonez. In the hotel room of Ordonez, Sharon ended up shooting him dead. She was now in prison for murder again, only this time in Mexico! Sharon Kinne said she shot Ordonez when he made sexual advances. "When I pushed him away, he hit me and then put his knee on my stomach. He hit me again several times. He covered my mouth so I couldn't scream, but I managed to throw him off and onto the floor. It gave me time to pull my gun from my purse. I fired – I don't know how many times, one or two times."

The Mexican courts didn't believe a word of Sharon's story and sentenced her to thirteen years in prison. In 1969, five years into her sentence, the 29 year-old Sharon Kinne managed to escape from her Mexican prison and that was the last anyone saw of her. No one knows where she went or what happened to her. She simply vanished. Sharon Kinne is therefore something of a mythic figure in true crime lore today. In Mexico she is known as La Pistolera - The Gunfighter.

(72) RHONDA BELL MARTIN (Years Active 1937-1951, Six Victims)

Rhonda Belle Martin was born in 1907. Martin was an Alabama waitress who confessed to poisoning to death several members of her family in 1956. She killed three daughters, her mother and two husbands, mostly with rat poison. Martin also attempted to kill her fifth husband (and former step-son) but he survived and was left a paraplegic. The authorities were rather befuddled as to why she became a serial poisoner of relatives because the life insurance money and inheritances she accrued from these deaths was modest and barely covered all the funeral expenses.

Rhonda Belle Martin never really offered an explanation as to why she had killed most of her family. It has been suggested that she became addicted to the attention and sympathy she received whenever a relative died. Rhonda Belle Martin was rumbled when her latest husband survived his poisoning. An investigation soon deduced that many relatives of Martin had been poisoned. She also used ant poison and arsenic to kill her relatives. The poison was often put in coffee and then served up to the victim.

Rhonda Belle Martin was a rather unlikely serial killer as she was a plump and conservative looking bespectacled middle-age housewife. Although she confessed to the murders her inability to explain why she had done them simply made her all the more baffling. Martin's lawyer tried to go for a plea of insanity in court and suggest that Rhonda had (as you do!) bumped off her husband so she could marry her step-son. In the end she was only tried for the death of her fourth husband. That was more than sufficient to give her the harshest of sentences.

It took a jury just over three hours to find her guilty. The sentence was death. Rhonda Belle Martin burst into tears at the verdict but was later quite stoic as her execution loomed. "Well, you've never seen anybody who was ready to sit down in the electric chair,' she said. 'But if that's what it's got to be, that's what it will be." She was executed in Alabama's electric chair on October 11, 1957. For her last meal she had a hamburger, mashed potatoes, cinnamon rolls and coffee.

Rhonda Belle Martin asked for her body to be donated to medical science in the hope that it might be of use in understanding future killers. 'At my death,' she wrote, 'whether it be a natural death of otherwise, I want my body to be given to some scientific institution to be used as they see fit, but especially to see if someone can find out why I committed the crimes I have committed. I can't understand it, for I had no reason whatsoever. There is definitely something wrong. Can't someone find it and save someone else the agony I have been through.'

(71) THE LOVE SLAVE KILLERS (Years Active 1978–1980, Ten Victims)

Gerald and Charlene Gallego became known as The Love Slave Killers in Sacramento, California. This was an unlikely duo. Gerald Gallego was a known criminal who once molested a child but Charlene Gallego was from a good family and intelligent. Nonetheless, they married and he exerted great control over her. Gerald Gallego's fantasy to was have 'love slaves' and Charlene facilitated this by helping him to lure victims to their van. Despite her best efforts to absolve herself from blame, there is no question that Charlene Gallego shares some responsibility for these awful crimes.

Gerald Gallego was born in 1946. His mother was a sex worker and his father was criminal who went to the gas chamber for killing a police officer. The cards dealt to Gerald Gallego as a child were rather hopeless. It wasn't a great start in life to say the least. He began a life of crime at the age of thirteen. Before too long he had racked up dozens of arrests. He was a thief, a child molester, and - in time - a murderer. He got married several times and at points in his life was married to more than one woman. Gerald Gallego was always a crazy and dangerous sort of character.

Charlene Gallego was born in 1956. She was said to have a stable family life but went off the rails as a teenager thanks to drugs and alcohol. She married a couple of times before she came into the awful orbit of Gerald Gallego. In 1978 Gerald Gallego raped and murdered two teenage girls that Charlene had found. He would kill five more people in 1980 - including one man. Gerald Gallego would rape the victims and then kill them by any means possible. Strangulation, gun, a hammer, shovel. It made no difference to him. The one male victim was shot (his girlfriend was then sexually abused). The bodies of the victims were usually buried in shallow graves that had been hastily dug.

Gerald and Charlene Gallego were thankfully captured in 1980. A friend of Craig Miller and Mary Elizabeth Sowers (who were the last victims) had witnessed their attack and abduction and thankfully had the presence of mind to write down the number plate of Gerald Gallego - which led to the arrest of this wicked couple. Once in custody, Charlene agreed to testify against Charlene Gallego as part of a plea bargain that would reduce her sentence. Gerald Gallego was sentenced to death at the trial but died in prison in 2002 while still on death row.

Charlene Gallego was already free by the time that her former husband died behind bars. She was released in 1997. Charlene Gallego was given a new identity for her release back into society. She had impressed the prison authorities by the way she studied in prison and gained more educational qualifications. Charlene Gallego later spoke to the media and said she had tried to save the victims and did not participate in any of the murders. She claimed that she had tried to get away from Gerald Gallego but it was impossible because he would have killed her. "There were victims who died, and there were victims who lived," she said. "It's taken me a hell of a long time to realize that I'm one of the ones who lived."

Many believe though that Charlene Gallego was released far too early. A lot of the relatives of the victims of The Love Slave Killers think that Charlene Gallego is a lot more guilty than she admits and should still be behind bars. Inmates who were in prison with her have said she secretly confessed that felt excited by the murders and there is evidence that she took a much fuller part in them than she ever confessed to. It was Charlene who lured the victims and thus Charlene who facilitated many of the awful things that happened - including, of course, murder.

(70) DANA SUE GRAY (Years Active 1994, Three Victims)

Dana Sue Gray was born Dana Sue Armbrust in 1957 in southern California. Dana Sue Gray worked as a nurse and killed three older women in a gated community in 1994. The ferocity of the attacks shocked the police. One victim was left with a knife sticking out of her neck and another was strangled with a telephone cord. The motivation of Dana Sue Gray was money. She was addicted to shopping and had run up debts. Gray was what you might describe as a shopaholic. Having no money to buy things made her feel miserable.

Gray seemed fairly normal as a young women. She was fond of skydiving and worked hard at nursing school. Gray also loved golf and would take trips to Hawaii to go golfing. She got married (to Tom Gray) in 1987 and the couple dabbled in several business ventures. The marriage didn't last long though and ended around 1993. Dana Sue Gray worked at Inland Valley Regional Medical Center as a nurse but she was fired for stealing painkillers. The business ventures she had with her former husband had practically bankrupted them by now too so things were looking bleak.

If there was one thing Dana hated more than anything else it was not having any money. She therefore resorted to murder to secure what she desired. The victims of Gray were vulnerable and elderly women who lived in the same Canyon Lake gated community that she did. The first victim was 86 year-old Norma Davis. Norma was found with a knife in her neck and a knife in her chest. Her social security cheques had been rifled through.

The next victim was 66 year-old June Roberts. Roberts knew Dana Sue Gray and was apparently helping her with alcohol addiction. Gray strangled Roberts with a telephone cord and stole two credit cards before going to a big shopping trip at the local mall. She treated the young son of her boyfriend to a meal, had a perm and manicure, then purchased some earrings, cowboy boots, a jacket, and some vodka. Gray even got some treats for her dog on the credit cards of the woman she had just murdered!

The last victim was 87 year-old Dora Beebe, who Gray attacked and killed in her usual fashion. Once again she went on a big spending spree with the credit cards she found in the victim's home. Unbelievably, Gray then tried to kill a woman named Dorinda Hawkins in an antiques store. Hawkins, who worked in the store, was helping Gray find some items when she suddenly felt some rope around her neck. Thankfully she managed to struggle and survive the attack.

Dana Sue Gray was eventually arrested for the credit card theft and - of course - murder. She tried to pretend that she had merely stolen the credit cards and hadn't killed anyone but that was obviously a lie. Gray told the police that she was simply addicted to shopping and buying things. It was the only thing that made her happy. Shopping made her so happy that she was perfectly willing to murder people to get the money to fund her hobby. In 1998 she was sentenced to life in prison. Dana Sue Gray pleaded guilty to avoid the death penalty and was incarcerated in the California Women's Prison in Chowchilla.

(69) ANNA MARIE HAHN (Years Active 193-1937, Five Victims)

Anna Marie Hahn was born Anna Marie Filse in Bavaria, Germany, in 1906. When she was still a teenager, Hahn had a child and claimed the father was a respected doctor. However, this respected doctor did not exist. It was something Hahn had made up to mitigate the stigma of being a single mother. Hahn's pregnancy with no marriage or husband was something of a scandal in the family and she was sent away to the United States in 1929. Anna Marie Hahn's family was fairly rich and conservative so you could say that they rather sent her into exile. She had become the black sheep of the clan.

Anna Marie ended up in Cincinnati, Ohio where she married a fellow German immigrant named Philip Hahn. They started a family together. Anna Marie is said to have briefly run a bakery but clearly didn't enjoy this much and it didn't last very long. Accounts of her life often say she had a number of gambling debts. One thing was certain in the end. Anna Marie Hahn liked money and would do literally anything to get her hands on it.

Alarm bells regarding the activities of Anna Marie first began to ring when she seemed unusually insistent that her husband should take out life insurance - despite the fact that he was quite young. Sure enough, her husband soon fell ill and was carted off to hospital (where he managed to survive) by relatives. With her marriage in tatters, Anna Marie took up a position caring for elderly men in Cincinnati's German community. You can probably guess what happened next. That's right. The elderly patients she was caring for soon began to suddenly and mysteriously die.

Anna Marie would borrow money from her patients before they died. One patient even left her a house in his will. She would earn their trust (and in some cases it seems even they love) before she poisoned them. The last victim was George Obendoerfer in 1937. Anna Marie plundered his bank account after she'd killed him. The police got suspicious of Anna Marie because of the bank transfer she had arranged so soon after the death of Obendoerfer. His body was found to contain poison - as were the bodies of her previous two patients after exhumations.

It transpired that Hahn was creative in her methods and used different poisons (including arsenic and croton oil) on different victims. A search of her home found a large stash of poison (in addition to belongings she had stolen from her victims) and she was taken into custody. After a four week trial, Anna Marie was sentenced to death. This came as a big shock to her. Anna Marie Hahn had been so confident of a not guilty verdict that she had her bags packed so that she was ready to go home. At the trial Anna Marie Hahn was cogent and well dressed and insisted she was innocent. The evidence though said otherwise.

As her execution loomed, Anna Marie became confessional

and composed a written statement. 'God above will tell me what made me do these terrible things,' she wrote. 'I couldn't have been in my right mind when I did them. I loved all people so much. Now I am so close to death. Death is all around me. I have been here (on death row) for what seems another lifetime already. Several other people in this place have been called out. I hope that God will take care of my son, for I would not want anything to happen to my boy. I feel that God has shown me my wrongs in life and my only regret is that I have not the power to undo the trouble and heartache that I have caused.' Anna Marie Hahn was executed by electrocution at the Ohio Penitentiary on December the 7th, 1938. Her son Oskar was given a new identity and served in the United States Navy during World War 2.

(68) VELMA BARFIELD (Years Active 1969-1978, Six Victims)

Velma Barfield was born in South Carolina in 1932. She had a pretty awful childhood by most accounts and there were stories that her father sexually abused her. At the age of seventeen, Velma got married and eventually had two children. She worked at a factory but didn't last long and was on a battery of prescription drugs. Her marriage was increasingly fractious and in 1969 she took her children and left her husband Thomas Burke.

The family home suspiciously burned down at this time - with Thomas Burke (who had passed out) still inside at the time. Not long afterwards, Velma married a man named Jennings Barfield. Less than a year into the marriage though, Barfield died. The cause of death was believed at the time to be a result of heart problems. He was said to have been having a lot of arguments though with Velma before his swift and unexpected demise.

In 1974, Velma's mother died after experiencing severe and painful stomach pains. Velma was employed as a caretaker around this time but the two couples she was employed to care for also suddenly and mysteriously died. Their symptoms were identical to those of Velma's late mother. You didn't need to be Columbo to suspect that death seemed to follow Velma Barfield around a little too much not to be highly suspicious. By now, Velma had acquired a boyfriend named Rowland Stuart Taylor. You can probably guess what happened to him. Before he died, Taylor had deduced that Velma had been forging his cheques.

After the death of Rowland Stuart Taylor, the police received a secretive tip that they should investigate Velma Barfield. Taylor's body was exhumed and found to contain arsenic. When the bodies of others who had died in the proximity of Velma Barfield were examined they were also found to contain arsenic. Velma was arrested and confessed to four murders. She was convicted and sentenced to death - despite objections from psychiatric witnesses who felt she was not of sound mind.

Velma Barfield became a Christian in prison and her last few years were spent ministering to prisoners. She also apologised for her crimes. It was all to no avail though as Governor Jim Hunt refused to grant a pardon. She was killed by lethal injection in 1984. Barfield had one of the more basic last meal requests as far as condemned prisoners go. For her last meal she simply asked for some Coca-Cola and a bag of Cheez Doodles.

(67) JOANNA DENNEHY (Years Active 2013, Three Victims)

Joanna Dennehy was born in 1982 in St Albans, Hertfordshire. Dennehy is a female serial killer who stabbed three men to death with a knife in England in 2013. Dennehy then tried to kill two other men who were out walking their dogs. She attacked both of these dog walkers but they managed to survive. Joanna Dennehy was a shocking case not only for the ruthless barbarity of her attacks but also because she came from a normal family. Dennehy seemed to go off the rails somewhat as a teenager. She left home at fifteen and dabbled in drugs. She then had two children at a very young age.

Dennehy was into self-harm and drank a lot. Her mental stability was clearly not on a firm footing. She served some time in juvenile detention for theft and her partner John Treanor took their children and left her. Dennehy was diagnosed with antisocial personality disorder and prescribed medication to curb her violent mood swings. In 2013, Dennehy began a relationship with a much older man named Kevin Lee in Peterborough. Lee supplied rooms to vulnerable people in need of cheap accommodation and Dennehy sort of became his bodyguard. She was the person he sent in when someone hadn't paid the rent.

In March 2013, Dennehy invited a 31-year-old Polish immigrant named Lucasz Slaboszewski to her flat and then stabbed him through the heart. She then got a criminal associate of hers named Gary 'Stretch' Richards to help her dispose of the body. The body was dumped in a ditch not too far away. Dennehy then called at the flat of 56 year-old neighbour John Chapman. After they drank alcohol together and Chapman eventually passed out drunk, Dennehy stabbed him in the chest several times. Once again, Gary Richards (and a criminal associate of his named Leslie Layton) helped to dispose of the body.

Dennehy's next victim was Kevin Lee. She stabbed him in the heart and his body was put in one of her dresses before being dumped in a public place. By now, Dennehy and Richards were obviously partners in crime. They staged a robbery together and Dennehy spoke of wanting to kill nine people to be like Bonnie and Clyde. She said she would only kill men though and wouldn't kill women. Richards drove Dennehy around to satisfy her request for more victims. They stopped the car at random and she jumped out to stab two men who were out walking their dogs. One of these men was stabbed thirty times but managed to survive.

Joanna Dennehy's bloodthirsty killing spree came to an end because Kevin Lee's relatives reported him as missing. When his body was discovered it didn't take Sherlock Holmes to deduce that Joanna Dennehy was someone who should be investigated. The two dog walkers who were stabbed by Dennehy also gave the police a description of their attacker. Dennehy was swiftly arrested. On the 8th of May 2013, Joanna Dennehy was charged with the murder of Kevin Lee and the attempted murders of (dog walkers) Robin Bereza and John Rogers.

Joanna Dennehy pleaded guilty in court (despite the objections of her defence team). She is only the third woman in Britain to receive a full life tariff after Myra Hindley and Rose West. She showed no remorse whatsoever for her crimes. Her accomplices Richards and Layton also received prison sentences. Dennehy said that killing someone was 'moreish' and that she got a taste for murder after her first one. She is a highly dangerous and disturbed women who will, thankfully, never see the light of day again.

(66) MYRA HINDLEY (Years Active 1963-1965, Five Victims)

Ian Brady and Myra Hindley became known as The Moors Murderers for abducting and killing children on Saddleworth Moor between 1963 and 1965. The awful crimes shocked Britain and still haunt the city of Manchester. The Moors Murders shocked Britain most of all because a woman was involved. Myra Hindley was born in Manchester in 1942. She had a fairly bog standard background and became a clerk at an engineering firm when she left school.

In 1961, Hindley got a job as a typist at Millwards Merchandising. It was here that she met the vile and much older Ian Brady. Brady was a thief who loved reading Mein

Kampf. Hindley was completely besotted with Brady and he would regale her with tales of the Marquis de Sade and Nazis. Hindley even stopped going to church because Brady told her that God didn't exist. The couple were soon planning bank robberies together and it's a great pity they didn't stick to that plan. What they did instead was indescribably evil and constituted the most harrowing crimes anyone could imagine.

In 1963 they abducted a sixteen year-old girl and murdered her. They then abducted twelve-year-old John Kilbride - who was raped by Brady and then had his throat slit before he was strangled. In 1964 they murdered twelve year-old Keith Bennett and ten-year-old Lesley Ann Downey. Lesley was forced to pose for nude photographs before she was killed. The evil duo would record the torture of the victims on audio tape and then bury the bodies on the bleak Saddleworth Moor. In 1965, Brady and Hindley killed seventen year-old Edward Evans with an axe. However this death was witnessed by David Smith, the husband of Hindley's younger sister.

Smith called the police and Brady was arrested. It took a little longer for Hindley to be implicated in this awful case. The evil duo ludicrously tried to pin the murder on Smith but the police found considerable evidence which stated otherwise. They found tape recordings of victims, photographs of Lesley Ann Downey, and even a picture of Hindley posing on John Kilbride's grave. The trial took place in April 1965 and both Brady and Hindley were found guilty of murder and given a life sentence. They were both fortunate that the death penalty had only recently been outlawed in England.

The Moors Murders were incredibly harrowing and upsetting for the general public at the time. You could say that society was less innocent in the 1960s. Crimes like this were simply far less reported and less prevalent too. The thought that a woman was involved in the torture and murder of children was beyond belief to society at the time. Ian Brady said that as a boy on his paper round he encountered the face of Death - who showed him the vision of children on a moor. Brady, in his own mind, saw the Moors Murders as a sacrificial offering to the 'Death' figure who had visited him as a child. Brady's childhood 'vision' is probably explained by the fact that he had a form of epilepsy which left him prone to hallucinations.

Myra Hindley would later blame Brady for the murders and said that she was fearful of him and was abused. In cases like this it is fairly common for the female half of the duo to claim they were a victim too and had no choice. "I had this obsession about him," said Hindley of Brady. "This infatuation, I believed it to be love. I think it stemmed from the fact Brady was so different to anyone I had met. He seemed cloaked in an aura of mystery I could never quite penetrate, never quite solve and this unknowability intrigued me and continued to enhance his attraction to me."

Despite her expressions of remorse and attempts to get parole, no one really believed that Hindley was innocent and she will probably forever be the most infamous female figure in British true crime history. There were attempts, especially by Lord Longford, to release Myra Hindley from prison but the newspapers and British public were appalled by this. Hindley died in prison in 2002. Myra Hindley was still so despised that when she died the prison authorities struggled to find an undertaker willing to handle the cremation.

(65) AMY ARCHER GILLIGAN (Years Active 1907–1917, 5+ Victims)

Amy Archer-Gilligan was born in Milton, Connecticut, in 1873. She was one of ten children and got married to a man named James Archer in 1897. In 1901 the couple became caretakers and were hired to look after a widower named John Seymour. Seymour died in 1904 and (after arranging rent with the Seymour estate) they converted his home into a boarding house for the elderly. The house was known as Sister Amy's Nursing Home for the Elderly. James Archer died in 1910. Amy had (rather suspiciously) taken out life insurance on him a few weeks before but he was in pretty poor health anyway so there didn't seem to be anything too dodgy about his demise.

In 1913, Amy married Michael W. Gilligan. However, he died only three months into the marriage and left his entire estate to Amy. Highly suspicious wouldn't you say? His death was classified as an attack of acid indigestion. It later transpired that Amy had forged his will so that he left his money to her rather than his sons. Around 1916, Amy Archer-Gilligan was known as Sister Amy in her nursing home for the elderly. She was a veritable Saint in the community. It was all a sham though - as was about to be revealed.

A man at the home named Franklin Andrews dropped dead one day while in the garden. His family were rather puzzled by this because he had seemed to be in excellent health. The family of the deceased man decided to investigate the home and do some detective work. They learned that Amy Archer-Gilligan had taken a $500 loan from Andrews just before he dropped dead. These findings were passed onto the authorities. It was the local newspaper though that took the most interest in the case.

The local newspaper learned that over fifty people had died in suspicious circumstances while in the care of Sister Amy. They also learned of the fact that Amy's two husbands had both died and left all of their money to her. As if that wasn't enough they also heard that Army often purchased large quantities of arsenic because she said she had a rat problem. When the newspaper (The Hartford Courant) began running stories about what they'd discovered, the authorities finally took action against Amy Archer-Gilligan.

It took a year to investigate the case but exhumations proved that Amy had been poisoning many of the tenants of her home to steal their money. It was also proven that Amy had poisoned her second husband. It took a jury only four hours to convict her. The death penalty was ruled out because she was deemed to be insane. Amy Archer-Gilligan was sent to a mental hospital in Middletown. She remained in this hospital until her death in 1962 at the age of 88. Though convicted of five counts of murder, Amy Archer-Gilligan almost certainly killed a lot more people than that.

(64) LYDIA SHERMAN (Years Active 1863–1877, Twelve Victims)

Lydia Sherman was born Lydia Danbury in Burlington, New Jersey in 1824. Lydia was yet another of those female poisoner serial killers. She was an orphan as a child and (as was custom at the time) got married when she was only a teenager. Her husband was a man named Edward Struck and the couple soon had children. In the 1860s, Lydia, obviously tired of family life, decided to take out some life insurance on her husband. She then went and purchased some rat poison. When her husband died as a result of poisoning, no one suspected a thing so Lydia took out insurance on her six children and killed them too.

In 1868, Lydia married a farmer named Dennis Hurlbrut. Dennis was said to be in quite poor health and on his last legs but Lydia was clearly not a patient woman because she poisoned him too. In April 1870, Lydia took a job as housekeeper to Nelson Sherman (from whom she got her name). Sherman had a baby son and teenage daughter. Lydia became a trusted part of this family (Nelson Sherman even planned to marry her) and then - once she had lulled them into a false sense of security - poisoned them all.

Nelson himself was dispatched by means of rat poison in a mug of hot chocolate. By now though, Lydia had pushed her luck as far as it would go. A local doctor found these deaths highly suspicious and conducted an investigation. Sure enough, arsenic was found in the bodies and Lydia was arrested. Lydia Sherman surprised people in court as she was a very prim and proper looking woman who seemed an unlikely serial killer. She was of fairly low intelligence though and couldn't read or write.

Lydia Sherman's defence tried to argue that she hadn't meant to kill these people and that Nelson Sherman might have taken his life because he was heartbroken at the death of his children. This defence didn't stand up to much scrutiny and Lydia Sherman was sentenced to life in prison for her heartless crimes. She was a remarkably cold and ruthless killer in the way that she had no qualms about targeting children. After her conviction she dictated a confession - which perhaps suggested she did have some flickers of humanity and remorse.

Lydia actually escaped from prison in 1977 and made her way to Providence, Rhode Island. She was soon captured though and died in prison several weeks later. In true crime circles, Lydia Sherman has attracted a number of sobriquets that include The Modern Lucretia Borgia, The Poison Fiend, The Borgia of Connecticut and The Queen Poisoner. Lydia Sherman died of cancer in 1878 at the age of 53. She was an exceptionally dangerous and calculating poisoner. No one was safe at all if they shared a house with Lydia Sherman. She is believed to have killed twelve people in all though some sources put the figure at ten. The real number of victims, as is often the case with serial killers, is difficult to verify for sure.

(63) CHRISTINE FALLING (Years Active 1980-1982, Six Victims)

Christine Falling was born in Florida in 1963. Falling had quite a difficult childhood as she suffered from epilepsy and was also said to have learning difficulties. Her family were also very poor so life was pretty tough at times. She spent some time in orphanages and was said to be quite disturbed. There is evidence that she was cruel to animals. This unforgivable behaviour is often cited as a sign that someone might be capable of becoming a serial killer one day. Anyone who is cruel to animals obviously has something seriously wrong with them. These people lack basic human compassion.

In 1977, Falling was manipulated into a marriage by her parents. She was only fourteen years-old. The marriage only lasted a few weeks. In her teens, Falling suffered from severe mental health problems and was prone to hallucinations. Despite her troubles, Falling picked up some money in her neighbourhood by working as a babysitter. Hiring Christine Falling as a babysitter turned out to be a tragic decision for a number of families.

Her first victim was a two-year girl. The post mortem indicated that the child had received a blow to the head but Falling said the baby had fallen from a crib. Although doctors were dubious about Falling's story this case (tragically as it turned out) wasn't investigated any further. Christine Falling moved to Florida thereafter and killed a four year-old boy she was caring for. His death was attributed to myocarditis. Falling actually babysat his little brother during the funeral but he died in her care too only days later. Amazingly, she still didn't attract any undue suspicion. The deaths of the brothers were believed to have been a result of a viral infection that was passed from one to the other.

In 1981, Falling returned to her home town and got a job caring for an elderly man. He lasted less than a day in the care of Christine Falling before passing away. Not long after, Christine's half-sister left her infant daughter in Falling's care while she went out to buy groceries. Sadly, you can probably imagine what happened next. The infant suddenly died while being cared for by Christine Falling. In July, 1982, a ten month old boy also died while under the care of Falling and an autopsy discovered the cause of death was suffocation. Christine Falling (not before time you might say) was finally spoken to by the police and confessed to murdering a number of children. She said that voices in her head from God had told her to commit these murders.

Because she confessed to her crimes, Falling evaded a death sentence and received life in prison. She was charged with three murders in the end. Though she killed more than three people the others were difficult to prove. Three was more than sufficient though to give her life in prison. "The way I done it, I seen it done on TV show," she said of her murders. "I had my own way, though. Simple and easy. No one would hear them scream." The case of Christine Falling is grim and harrowing indeed. This was a woman who should have triggered alarm bells much sooner. It is a great tragedy that no one took Falling out of society sooner and made sure she wasn't a danger to the public.

(62) ELIZABETH WETTLAUFER (Years Active 2007-2017, Eight Victims)

Elizabeth Wettlaufer was born on Ontario, Canada in 1967. She studied nursing as a young woman and was eventually employed in a care home. Her time at Caressant Care though was plagued by problems related to her drug and alcohol addictions. She was eventually fired for various infractions - which included getting medications mixed up and being found passed out drunk in a storeroom. Wettlaufer was then employed at the Meadow Park Care Center but her time there was cut short when she had to have treatment for her drug problems.

After this Wettlaufer had a battery of medical positions in different places but - once again - never lasted very long. She was caught stealing from one care home and her habit of turning up for work drunk or high meant she was not a very reliable employee to say the least. The last thing a medical business (not to mention the patients) needs is the nurses turning up to work drunk or high on drugs. This was only the tip of the iceberg though. Turning up for work drunk or stealing was one thing but Wettlaufer was also trying to kill patients with injections of insulin.

Her first murder is believed to have occurred in 2007 when she killed a World War 2 veteran who was being looked after at Caressant Care. Elizabeth Wettlaufer killed eight patients in various places and attempted to kill a further six. In 2016, Wettlaufer checked into a drug rehabilitation centre and confessed to her crimes. She said the motivation for the murders was a strange 'surge' and compulsion which she couldn't control. Wettlaufer said that when this surge gripped her she could hear cackling laughter which seemed to be coming from the bowels of hell. Elizabeth Wettlaufer was clearly highly disturbed and just about the last person in the world you'd want working in a medical care home.

Staff who worked with Wettlaufer later said she was a friendly woman who would often bring the patients gifts. They had no idea that she was secretly killing them. Wettlaufer, like other Angel of Mercy medical killers, was said to be obsessed with death and intoxicated with the power she had over the fate of her patients. She had this deluded sense that she was sparing people from pain by killing them.

Wettlaufer was charged formally with eight counts of murder and (later) six more charges consisting of four counts of attempted murder and two counts of aggravated assault. Elizabeth Wettlaufer was then sentenced to life imprisonment and later sent to a secure facility in Montreal to receive medical treatment. In a report on the case, Commissioner Eileen E. Gillese admitted that Elizabeth Wettlaufer might not have been caught if she hadn't confessed (which was a rather disturbing admission). 'The evidence,' said Gillese, 'showed that no one suspected that Wettlaufer was intentionally harming those under her care — not the residents or their families, not those who worked alongside Wettlaufer, and not those who managed and supervised her.'

Elizabeth Wettlaufer was found to be suffering from antisocial personality disorder and is believed to have killed the patients purely for her own gratification. Ultimately, this was a highly disturbed and troubled woman who couldn't seem to distinguish right from wrong anymore. If she hadn't been caught there is no telling how many people she might have killed in the end. This case received much publicity in Canada because it was revealed that Wettlaufer's previous infractions at medical facilities were not reported to the College of Nurses of Ontario. If they had been she might have been banned from working as a nurse much sooner and thus prevented some of these tragedies.

(61) HILDA NILSSON (Years Active 1915-1917, Convicted of Eight Murders, Suspected of Other Murders)

Hilda Nilsson was born in Helsingborg, Sweden in 1876. Nilson was another of those awful baby farmer killers. She turned to baby farming as a way to make money after running up a number of debts. Because she came across as a normal and sincere woman and her house was very clean and tidy, no one detected any sense of danger from her and were perfectly willing to leave babies in her charge. This turned out to be a tragic mistake.

Baby farming flourished in this era because it was considered to be a great sin in society for an unmarried woman to have a child. As a consequence there were always plenty of unwanted illegitimate babies. Only two of the children entrusted to Hlda Nilsson survived. She was disturbingly hands on in the fashion in which she killed the children. She would put the babies in the bath and then place a heavy object over them until they drowned. Nilsson would then either bury or burn the body.

The remarkable thing about this case is that Hilda Nilsson was married and yet her husband genuinely had no idea that she was killing the infants they looked after. If he ever inquired why one of the infants was missing, Hilda Nilsson would tell him that they had been found a home. Hilda Nilsson was rumbled when a woman named Blenda Henricsson decided she wanted to visit the son she had entrusted to Hilda. Hilda told Blenda that the child had gone away to live with Hilda's sister. However, Hilda could provide no address for her sister.

Blenda persisted and visited Hilda again but this time Hilda said the child had died - which completely contradicted her claim of the infant staying with her sister. After a little digging, Blenda Henricsson (who was by now understandably suspicious) discovered that Hilda Nilsson didn't actually have a sister. Hilda had been feeding her a pack of lies. Blenda Henricsson contacted the Foster Children's Board - who in turn turned the matter over to the police.

Hilda was arrested and sentenced to death by guillotine. However, Hilda killed herself in prison before the execution took place. In a quirk of fate her death sentence had been reduced to life in prison but she wasn't aware of this yet when she killed herself. At her trial, Hilda Nilsson had admitted giving infants opium so that they would make less noise. Unsurprisingly, the laws on adoption in Sweden were changed soon after this case in order to protect fostered children and infants from the likes of Hilda Nilsson. She was a cold and wicked woman indeed.

(60) DELPHINE LALAURIE (Years Active 1831-1834, Many Suspected Victims)

Delphine LaLaurie was born in New Orleans, Spanish Louisiana in 1787. She was a socialite who has become a notorious figure for her alleged torture and murder of many slaves who served in her household. The story of Delphine LaLaurie is much disputed today. No one is quite sure how much of her story is folklore and how much is true. The story goes that in 1834 there was a huge fire in her mansion. The people who responded to his fire discovered a torture room in the attic where all manner of grisly sights awaited them.

Author Jeanne deLavigne described the scene in her book Ghost Stories of Old New Orleans - 'Male slaves, stark naked, chained to the wall, their eyes gouged out, their fingernails pulled off by the roots; others had their joints skinned and festering, great holes in their buttocks where the flesh had been sliced away, their ears hanging by shreds, their lips sewn together... Intestines were pulled out and knotted around naked waists. There were holes in skulls, where a rough stick had been inserted to stir the brains.'

Vice wrote of this alleged attic of horror - 'A brief catalogue of the ever-changing list of horrors people claim the would-be rescuers found in her attic include: Heaps of corpses, organs, and limbs. Slaves pinned to tables or cramped in small cages. Live bodies with their eyes gouged, fingernails torn out, ears hanging by shreds of skin, or their mouths filled with animal shit and sewn shut. People flayed of skin with festering wounds. Many accounts claim they found one woman whose skin had been peeled off in spirals to make her look like a caterpillar, another with her bones broken and reset so that she looked like a crab, and one more whose intestines had been torn out and knotted around the waist. Many of these victims (some claim there were up to 100) were supposedly still alive—putrid and starving.'

The fire, according to the legend, was started by a disgruntled slave who was tired of the abuse going on at the mansion. Upon hearing about the ghastly goings on at the mansion of Delphine LaLaurie, locals are said to have descended on the house in a show of mob violence. They wanted to punish Delphine LaLaurie for her mistreatment of slaves. However, she managed to flee from the mob and escape justice of any kind. She vanished.

Not much is known about what happened to Delphine LaLaurie after this. Many accounts of the story of Delphine LaLaurie say that she escaped and made her way to France. Clearly, if one takes the legend of Delphine LaLaurie at face value then she was a serial killer of sorts and killed many people. It is difficult though to separate fact from fiction. There are enough accounts to suggest that she did have a cruel streak and mistreated slaves but some of the descriptions of her torture activities (one of which we noted a few paragraphs above) are clearly embellished and unverified. The truth is that we don't really know how many people Delphine LaLaurie killed and we don't know what really went on in that New Orleans mansion.

There is enough evidence to suggest though that Delphine LaLaurie was a very dangerous woman who you really wouldn't want to work for. One could argue that the story of Delphine LaLaurie is rather like that of The Bloody Benders. A fun grisly ghost story and piece of folklore that has elements of truth - as opposed to a factual case where we can verify facts from historical documents and reports from the trial. It seems that a lot of nasty stuff went on in the mansion of Delphine LaLaurie and history left her with an awful reputation but some of the details remain frustratingly vague. It seems fairly safe to say though that Delphine LaLaurie was no beloved figure or Saint. She was a notorious figure who was famed for her immense cruelty.

(59) JUDY BEUNOANO (Years Active 1971-1983, At Least Three Victims)

Judy Buenoano was born Judias Welty in Quanah, Texas in 1943. Judy Buenoano was known as The Black Widow. She poisoned her husband, drowned her son, and tried to kill her lover with a bomb! Judy, as is so often the case with killers and serial murderers, had a fairly lousy childhood. She was put up for adoption and suffered abuse from both her stepmother and stepfather. At the tender age of fourteen she got a short prison sentence for attacking her step-parents. Judy Buenoano was obviously someone who could only be pushed so far.

Rather than go back to her adopted family (who she clearly despised), Judy chose to go to reform school when her criminal sentence had ended. She left at the age of sixteen and got a job as a nursing assistant in Roswell. She became a mother soon after to a son named Michael Schultz. In 1962 she married an air force officer named James Goodyear and had two more children. She also had a business venture in the form of the Conway Acres Child Care Center in Orlando. James Goodyear died in 1971 of a mysterious illness and Judy cashed in his three life insurance policies. No, nothing suspicious about that at all! She then engineered a house fire to get more insurance money.

Soon after, Judy got a new boyfriend named Bobby Joe Morris. The couple moved to Colerado in 1972 but not before another suspicious house fire occurred. In 1978, Bobby Joe Morris died of a mysterious illness and Judy collected a generous life insurance payout. Judy changed her name to Buenoano (Judy had gone by a battery of various names in the past) around this time and moved back to Pensacola. Judy's son Michael Buenoano had joined the army by this time but he then suffered from very poor health. Michael suffered from paraplegia and wore leg braces. There were signs that suggested someone might be poisoning him.

In 1980, Michael went on a canoe trip with Judy and his brother James. After the canoe got into trouble he was left to fend for himself and ended up drowning because his leg braces were essentially like weights and made him sink. Judy told the authorities it had all been a complete accident and promptly collected Michael's military insurance payout. Judi now opened a beauty salon in Gulf Breeze and began dating a businessman named John Gentry II. By now though, the authorities were starting to become more than a little suspicious of Judy Buenoano. They found it rather odd that Michael had had three life insurance policies taken out on him shortly before he died. They also found evidence that signatures on these policies might have been forged.

Judy Buenoano had told John Gentry a pack of lies about her past. She claimed to be a nurse from Florida. Judy also insisted that they take out life insurance policies on one another. Another thing that Judy insisted on was that that Gentry should should improve his health by taking some special vitamin tablets she recommended. When these tablets made him feel ill she said he should increase the dose. It was pretty obvious in hindsight that these special tablets of Judy were not vitamin pills at all.

In 1983, Judy upped the ante from poisoning and strange canoeing accidents when she put a bomb in Gentry's car! The police found out that Judy had been going around telling friends that Gentry had a terminal illness and would be dead soon. After a complicated investigation they managed to link Judy to the bomb in Gentry's car. The bodies of Michael Goodyear, James Goodyear, and Bobby Joe Morris were all exhumed and found to contain arsenic. In 1984, Buenoano was convicted for the murder of Michael and the attempted murder of Gentry. In 1985 she was convicted of the murder of James Goodyear. Judy Buenoano went to the electric chair in 1998. For her last meal, she chose asparagus, strawberries, broccoli, tomatoes, and hot tea.

(58) DELLA SORENSON (Years Active 1918-1924, Eight Victims)

Della Sorenson was born in 1897. Between 1918 and 1923, Sorenson killed several people - all of whom were related to her. The murders took place in Howard County, Nebraska. Sorenson was only in her twenties when her crimes came to light. Della Sorenson was another of those infamous poisoners. All of her victims were poisoned. The first victim was her one-year-old niece, Viola Cooper, in 1918. Sorenson said she killed this child as revenge because she'd fallen out with Viola's mother. That gives you some idea of Sorenson's mental state. She was willing to murder someone's child just because she'd had an argument with them.

Two years later Sorenson murdered her own husband and then killed her mother-in-law. Sorenson is also believed to have murdered three of her own children and attempted (unsuccessfully) to murder two others. When she attempted to kill her second husband, Della Sorenson finally attracted the sort of suspicion and scrutiny one might expect and she was arrested in 1925. Once in custody she confessed to the murders.

The most bewildering part of this crime is that no real motivation for the deaths was readily apparent. It's not as if Sorenson made any money by killing all of these relatives. Della Sorenson simply said that she enjoyed killing and always felt a surge of elation and happiness after she had poisoned someone to death. She never expressed any remorse for her crimes at all. The gravity of what she had done didn't seem to register at all for Della Sorenson. She just didn't care.

The chilling thing about this case was the way Sorenson would give trivial reasons for why she had killed. She said she murdered one child after it kept crying. She wafted away the murder of a husband by saying they'd had an argument. She even said that she killed people because she enjoyed a good funeral. "I like to attend funerals," she told the police. "I'm happy when someone is dying." All of the murders took place in Sorenson's modest home. The relatives clearly detected no danger from her at all and trusted her.

Della, in her own warped imagination, seemed to think that these relatives had somehow deserved their tragic deaths. Sorenson was apparently rumbled when she gave two child relatives strychnine-laced candy but they managed to survive. She was deemed schizophrenic and sent to the state mental asylum. Della Sorenson was clearly a very troubled woman and it came as no surprise that the authorities deemed her to be too mentally unsound for a trial. She died in 1941.

(57) JAROSLAVA FABIANOVA (Years Active 1981-2003, Four Victims)

Jaroslava Fabiánová is a Czech serial killer born in 1965 in Děčín. Like most serial killers she had an unpleasant childhood and suffered sexual abuse. In the early 1980s she

joined a gang who took part in theft and prostitution.
Fabiánová began her life of crime as a thief and took part in
burglaries. She was lesbian in real life but had male clients in
her duties as a prostitute. It was for the murder of some of
these clients that she became an infamous figure in Czech true
crime circles.

One can see why Jaroslava Fabiánová is sometimes dubbed
the Czech Aileen Wuornos. Fabiánová, who was blonde and
rather haggard looking, even resembled Wuornos somewhat in
her appearance. Her first victim was a 78 year-old man who
had visited Fabiánová for sexual services but then tried to
avoid giving her any money. Fabiánová struck him three times
with a hammer and then stabbed him over twenty times. It
was a very frenzied and violent attack. Fabiánová was arrested
for the murder but because of her age (she was not yet a legal
adult) she only served four years in prison.

Upon her release, Fabiánová went back to prostitution and
would often rob her clients. These included a number of
foreign tourists. This sort of sideline was not quite as risky as it
might sound because if you were a foreign tourist who has
been robbed by a prostitute you probably wouldn't necessarily
want to report it to the police for all manner of reasons-
legality and embarrassment being the most obvious.

Fabiánová landed in prison again after drugging a client so she
could steal his money. The man died of cardiac arrest as a
result of the drugs she'd put in his drink. She was sentenced to
ten years in prison but, once again, got off quite lightly and
only served about five years in the end. Unbelievably, she is
said to have then served another short prison sentence for
stealing a telephone. Jaroslava Fabiánová was the ultimate
jailbird.

In 2003, Jaroslava Fabiánová went back to her old murderous
ways when she killed an elderly man named Augustin Kůra in
his apartment. He had been struck with a meat cleaver and
Fabiánová had then stolen some paintings and valuable tools

from his home. Fabiánová was stupid enough to try and sell
the paintings herself and this began the process of putting the
police onto her. Fabiánová then met a man named Richard
Sýkora on a tram. He invited Fabiánová to his home and she
stabbed him nearly forty times. She was pretty out of control
by this time and highly dangerous.

By now a search warrant had been put out for Fabiánová and
when the body of Richard Sýkora was discovered her DNA was
found on his fingernails. In 2005, despite her ludicrous claims
of innocence, Jaroslava Fabiánová was sentenced to life in
prison. She was only the third woman in the history of the
Czech Republic to be sentenced to life.

Jaroslava Fabiánová was described as intelligent by the
authorities after her conviction and she gave a confident (if
futile) performance in court. Experts judged her to be
egocentric and suffering from various personality disorders.
You could argue that Jaroslava Fabiánová, like Aileen
Wuornos, was a financially motivated killer. However,
Jaroslava Fabiánová seemed to take more pleasure in the act
of killing than Wuornos. She was certainly more gruesome in
her methods too.

(56) AILEEN WUORNOS (Years Active 1989–1990, Seven Verified Victims)

Aileen Wuornos was born in Rochester, Michigan, in 1956.
Wuornos is another serial killer who was born under a full
moon. Wuornos is arguably the most famous female serial
killer - mostly thanks to a film and documentary which were
made about her crimes. Charlize Theron won an Oscar for
portraying Aileen Wuornos in the 2003 film Monster.
Wuornos killed seven men in total from 1989 to 1990. She had
a tough start in life and an abusive upbringing at the hands of
a strict grandfather. Wuornos was a surprisingly beautiful
child but a tough life obviously extracted a cruel toll on her
looks in the end. She was homeless at fifteen and sold her body

to survive. Tired of the cold, she eventually hitchhiked to Florida and married a rich man. The marriage only lasted days. He put a restraining order on her because Wuornos would beat him up. Aileen Wuornos was a notoriously volatile person with an unpredictable (and rather frightening) temper.

After her marriage collapsed, Aileen Wuornos worked as a prostitute and, in desperate need of money, turned to murder. She picked up her victims on the I-75 highway. She would always target middle-aged men in nice cars. Once she was picked up, Wuornos would start to undress in the car and ask the driver to pull over somewhere secluded. Then she would get out of the car and shoot them before stealing their wallets. Aileen Wuornos would often shoot her victims multiple times.

Her alleged motivation for the murders was that she wanted to support her girlfriend and lover Ty. One might argue that a hatred of men was rather evident too. Psychologist Marissa Harrison concluded from her study that female serial killers were mostly motivated by material gain whereas male serial killers were mostly motivated by sexual urges. Aileen Wuornos was clearly motivated by her desperate desire to get quick money. Wuornos never really did much to hide the bodies of the victims. They were found fairly quickly and easily. A few men had a lucky escape from Aileen Wuornos. One man actually saw the gun in her purse and managed to drive away wile she was outside the vehicle.

Aileen Wuornos was captured when the police finally managed to get an accurate artists impression of the killer who was shooting these motorists. Once this sketch was circulated, they soon had a lot of calls telling them the illustration looked a lot like Aileen Wuornos - an angry and violent local woman who seemed to spend most of her spare time drinking beer in biker bars. Wuornos was taken into custody and the police discovered that she had sold the belongings (like wristwatches and jewelry) of the victims in local pawn shops. Any money they had she of course kept for herself.

Aileen Wuornos claimed that she had killed the men in self-defence because they all tried to rape her. This was seen as a weak and highly improbable defence. It appeared very unlikely that seven different men all tried to rape her at different times on the exact same stretch of highway. One of the victims was selling Bibles and another was a former police chief. They were ordinary people with no criminal history. The fact that Wuornos had not reported a single one of these incidents and always tried to hide the bodies also made her rape defence seem less than plausible.

Aileen Wuornos eventually pleaded guilty to five murders because she wanted the death penalty. She was tired of prison and court hearings. Aileen Wuornos felt betrayed and alone in the end. Even her beloved girlfriend Ty secretly taped their phone conversations and testified against her. Wuornos became a born again Christian after her conviction. She always got offended when someone called her a serial killer. Wuornos claimed she was not a serial killer because she never tortured or mutilated her victims. While this was true she did shoot dead several innocent men!

Aileen Wuornos was executed in 2002. Wuornos declined a last meal before her excecution and simply asked for black coffee. For $15 on crime collectible websites you can buy a photograph of Aileen Wuornos posing with a friend before her execution. She looks surprisingly happy in the photo considering the circumstances in which it was taken. Aileen Wuornos was a twist on the common serial killer situation in that she was a prostitute but a killer rather than a victim. She said she wasn't evil but just had a consuming hatred for the human race.

(55) VICKIE DAWN JACKSON (Years Active 2000-2001, 10+ Victims)

Vickie Dawn Jackson was born in 1966. In 2006 she pleaded no contest to charges that she had murdered ten patients at

Nocona General Hospital in Texas. Jackson worked as a vocational nurse at the hospital and would use an overdose of Mivacron (a muscle relaxant) to kill the patients. Jackson had always wanted to be a nurse and worked hard to pass her exams. However her daughter later said that Vickie Dawn Jackson was always a strange and unpredictable woman prone to rages. She didn't seem surprised at all to learn that her mother had been killing patients.

The hospital Jackson worked in was very small and so the workers there were on intimate terms with their patients. Over the course of 2000 and 2001, twenty patients died on the ward during the night shifts covered by Jackson. In that same time frame, not a single patient died during the night shifts not covered by Jackson. A lot of these patients were in the hospital for very minor conditions or injuries so the deaths were obviously suspicious to say the least.

In 2002 it was discovered that twenty bottles of Mivacurium had gone missing at the hospital. Syringes with traces of this drug were found in Jackson's trash. Exhumations of the patients who had died then revealed Mivacurium overdoses as the cause of death. The hospital had been subject to a negligence lawsuit from relatives of those that had died there in the past but Jackson kept working throughout this time.

What was especially chilling about Jackson's activities is that she targeted a number of people who she thought had slighted her. She tried to kill one patient who had called her fat and also killed her estranged husband's grandfather. The motivation for some these murders was petty to say the least. Jackson was arrested in 2002. After a mistrial (caused by a prosecutor's comments) she pleaded no contest in 2006. Jackson received life in prison for ten murders.

Not all of Vickie Dawn Jackson's victims were named due to privacy laws. Jackson clearly killed many more than ten patients but identifying how many is very complicated. Vickie Dawn Jackson never admitted any guilt and never offered any explanation as to why she killed these patients. It is believed that she pled no contest because her daughter was going to testify against her and say she was a dreadful mother. Vickie Dawn Jackson knew that she was going to be convicted whatever happened at the trial so she simply decided to cut to the chase and avoid the trial altogether.

(54) SARAH JANE ROBINSON (Years Active 1881–1886, Eleven Suspected Victims)

Sarah Jane Robinson was born in Ireland in 1838. When she was in her early teens her family moved to the United States. She married a man named Moses Robinson in 1858 and they lived in Sherborn, Massachusetts. Robinson is said to have met a man named Thomas R. Smith at the local church though and Smith became something of an accomplice in the awful crimes that followed. From 1881 onwards, members of the Robinson family began to fall ill with agonising stomach pains. It was naturally (and suspiciously) Sarah Jane Robinson who cared for these ill relatives. She was the one in charge of the medicine cabinet.

Nearly all of the ill (and soon to expire) relatives had life insurance through The Order of Pilgrim Fathers. The Order of Pilgrim Fathers was a local social group which offered affordable insurance to those who weren't wealthy. Sarah Jane took full advantage of this affordable insurance scheme in the deadliest way possible. Money was the primary motivation for her murders. She even poisoned the family's landlord and then tried to charge his family a fee for her 'nursing' services! She is alleged to have also stolen money from him.

As you might imagine, with all these relatives popping their clogs and the life insurance all going to Sarah Jane, it was only a matter of time before suspicion began to rear its head. Robinson was incredibly ruthless. She even killed her daughter and a seven year-old nephew. Sarah Jane was caught when her son William died but seemed to blame his mother for his illness before he passed away. The accusations of William were enough for a doctor to have tests done on his stomach tissue at a university after he died. This test established that William had been killed by arsenic poisoning.

Sarah Jane and two alleged accomplices (including of course Thomas R. Smith) were arrested. Further exhumations and tests confirmed that numerous Robinson family members (and their landlord to boot) had been poisoned. Sarah Jane pretended to be insane at first in an effort to dodge a trial and serious charges but this ruse was quickly seen through. She was originally sentenced to death but this was then commuted to life in prison. A year after the case a family who had moved into the old Robinson family home found a big box of rat poison hidden up the fireplace. Sarah Jane's guilt was never in question. She died in prison in 1906 at the age of 67. Robinson would become known as The Boston Borgia for her crimes.

(53) SOFIA ZHUKOVA (Years Active 2005-2019, Three Victims)

Sofia Zhukova was born in 1939 in the Soviet village of Zvyagino. She got married, had children, and worked on farms. There was nothing especially strange or odd about Sofia Zhukova it seemed. That all seemed to change after the death of husband in 2005. At this point, Zhukova made a surprising career change and became a serial killer. The first victim was Anastasia Alexeenko in 2005. Anastasia was an eight year-old girl who lived near Sofia Zhukova. Zhukova said she became irritated by the girl constantly making noise so she killed the child with an axe and then chopped the body up and dumped the remains in the street. Anastasia Alexeenko's severed head was later found near Sofia Zhukova's apartment.

The next victim was 77-year-old Anastasia Mikheyeva in 2017. Mikheyeva was a friend of Sofia Zhukova and staying at her apartment. Sofia Zhukova killed Mikheyeva in much the same fashion as she did the little girl and then chopped the body up.

The last victim was 57-year-old janitor Vasily Shlyakhtich in 2019. Shlyakhtich was renting a room from Sofia Zhukova when he was axed to death. His body was then dismembered and put on a rubbish dump. A severed arm was later found on the dump and it was reported that dogs ate some of the remains.

Sofia Zhukova said she killed Shlyakhtich because he made sexual advances towards her. This is possible but she was 80 years-old at the time so some doubt about this claim unavoidably exists. It seems just as likely that Sofia Zhukova was simply insane and quite enjoyed killing people. When the remains of these victims were discovered and identified the police didn't need to be Sherlock Holmes to connect them to Sofia Zhukova. They found numerous blood stains in her apartment and she was arrested. Sofia Zhukova died of the coronavirus at the end of 2020 but was then found guilty posthumously. Her advanced age alone made her a strange novelty sort of serial killer.

It was later reported that the organs of Zhukova's victims were found in her fridge - which obviously led to speculation that she was a cannibal. Locals told the newspapers that she would often bring them gifts of jellied meat and give the local children sweets. It is then alleged that Sofia Zhukova used her victims in these sweets. Sofia Zhukova is generally known as The Russian Granny Ripper today in true crime articles. She was a very cold and heartless woman who committed some awful crimes. It didn't come as a surprise to learn that Zhukova slaughtered animals when she worked on the farm. Anyone involved in the meat industry is obviously pretty cold and heartless to begin with.

(52) TIMEA FALUDI (Years Active 2000-2001, 30+ Victims)

Timea Faludi was born in Hungary in 1977. She was a nurse at the Gyula Nviro Hospital in Budapest and was convicted of murdering dozens of patients. Faludi joined the staff in 1994 and the deaths occurred during the night shifts she worked. She worked at the hospital for six years without raising any alarms and mostly cared for patients who were terminally ill. Faludi became an experienced nurse who was well liked by her colleagues and seemed very professional and good at her job. This all changed though when a colleague saw Faludi giving patients intravenous injections without a doctor's prescription.

Euthanasia is illegal in Hungary and she was arrested. Faludi confessed to killing forty patients when she was arrested but then seemed to retract this confession. The authorities could only find evidence for around ten deaths (a lot of the victims had obviously been cremated) - although it seems to be a fairly agreed fact that she killed a lot more people than that.

Faludi claimed that she killed because she wanted to relieve the suffering of patients but prosecutors begged to differ and believed that, like other medical killers, Faludi had developed a God complex and become intoxicated with the power she had over the life and death of patients. Faludi's crimes were mitigated by the fact that the patients she killed were apparently terminally ill. It is for this reason that she received a fairly light sentence of nine years (and was of course banned from ever becoming a nurse again). Was she a cold blooded killer or pure Angel of Mercy?

The case against Faludi would point out that her evidence was full of contradictions because she kept changing it (it seems plausible that her lawyers were the main culprits in this). There is also the fact that the patients she killed, while they might have been ill, did not give their consent for their lives to be terminated (in many cases they were incapable of this). Would Faludi have killed if she had been caring for non terminal patients? We may already know the answer to that question because two of her victims were not terminally ill and simply waiting for surgery.

The court verdict on Faludi stated that - "She alternately put herself in the place of the doctor or in that of the patient and took decisions instead of them. The term euthanasia can only be used at all if a patient expresses a wish to have his or her life terminated. In Faludi's cases, this did not happen." The court called Faludi a rational intelligent women who was trustworthy on the surface but secretly believed she was God. Faludi, who was 25 at the time of the trial, tends to be known as The Black Angel in Hungary. She was released from prison in 2009 and (understandably) maintains a low profile these days.

(51) GENENE JONES (Years Active 1970-1982, Two Verified Victims, 40+ Suspected Victims)

Genene Jones was born in Texas in 1950. She was adopted as a child and worked as a beautician before deciding to go to nursing school. Jones also got married and had children of her own. She eventually worked as a licensed vocational nurse (LVN) at the Bexar County Hospital (now University Hospital of San Antonio) in the pediatric intensive care unit. However, an unusually large number of children seemed to die during her shifts. Jones would inject digoxin, heparin, and other drugs into patients to induce a medical emergency.
She would then swoop in to revive them. Tragically a number of children because of this.

A motive for these murders was never established but Genene Jones, like all 'Angel of Death' medical killers, apparently developed a God complex. She was exhilarated by the power that she had over life and death and had become addicted to the practice of taking a child to the brink of death and then resuscitating them. Nurses who worked with her later recalled that Jones seemed to get strangely excited when a patient fell ill and even used to offer predictions on when the patient in question might expire.

It is impossible to say how many children she killed through her activities. Though she was convicted of two murders, fresh charges arrive to this day and a conservative estimate would put the number of victims around forty at the very least. The Bexar County Hospital was aware of the high number of deaths and feared a lawsuit so they simply dismissed all the licensed vocational nurses and replaced them with registered nurses. They also shredded medical records to protect themselves. The loss of these records later made prosecuting Genene Jones more complicated than it should have been.

After the Bexar County Hospital dismissed their nurses, Genene Jones soon got a job at a pediatrician's clinic in Kerrville, Texas. Once again though she was soon up to her old tricks. A doctor there found a puncture in a bottle of succinylcholine which only Jones had access to out of all the nurses. Succinylcholine is a medication used to cause short-term paralysis as part of general anesthesia. People under the influence of this drug can't breathe. Chelsea McClellan, a baby at the clinic, had died after Jones gave her some shots. Jones is believed to have killed around six children at this clinic.

Jones tried to use an insanity defence as her trial loomed but this didn't wash. The prosecution proved that she was perfectly sane and knew exactly what she was doing when she killed those patients. In 1985, Jones was sentenced to 99 years in prison for killing 15-month-old Chelsea McClellan with succinylcholine. In the second trial (for another hospital), she received 60 years. Genene Jones was indicted on new charges in recent years - which ended any lingering hopes she might have had of parole or freedom one day. In 2020, Jones pleaded guilty to causing the death of an eleven month old bay who had been under her care in 1981.

(50) ROSE WEST (Years Active 1971-1987, Ten Suspected Victims)

25 Cromwell Street in Gloucester became an infamous address in English criminal history thanks to the barely believable antics of Fred and Rose West. This bizarre couple were

involved in murder (which included some of their own children), prostitution, incest, and rape. Rose West claimed to be innocent but this was never credible. She was actually vital in allowing Fred West to pick up a number of victims. The presence of a wife made him seem like a normal (as far as the werewolf like Fred West could ever appear normal) person rather than a conspicuous threat. It was proven that Charmaine, the daughter of Fred and Rose, was murdered while Fred West was in prison. Rose West is believed to have killed more than one person and was clearly an accomplice. There were bodies under the patio and in the cellar at 25 Cromwell Street so it seems absolutely risible to think Rose West knew nothing of this.

Rosemary "Rose" Letts was born in Devon on November 29, 1953. Her father was a paranoid schizophrenic and her home life was difficult. Rose was deemed to be of below average intelligence at school. Rose's father greatly disapproved of her relationship with the twelve years older Fred West. This infamous couple met in 1968 when Rose was sixteen. It was later said that Rose West's father used to sexually abuse her. She would later say that other family relatives also abused her. Rose was unpredictable and had a violent temper. It is believed that she murdered 8-year-old Charmaine, Fred West's eldest child, in 1971.

Fred and Rose were married in 1972 and moved to 25 Cromwell Street. This was a three floor house with a cellar and back garden. The cellar of 25 Cromwell Street was (no surprise here) turned into a sex dungeon by Fred West. In 1972, Caroline Owens was hired as a babysitter by Fred and Rose West. She said she blacked out and woke up to find Fred West binding her with tape. She escaped and went to the police but they didn't seem to believe her story. Fred West escaped with a mild slap on the wrist because Owens was so scared of him she refused to take the Wests to court.

The Wests took in some lodgers around this time. Fred West (unsurprisingly) drilled peep holes into his walls so he could spy on the lodgers. West was also sexually abusing his daughters. The West children went to the hospital dozens of times for injuries they had sustained. One of the victims of Fred and Rose West around this time was Lucy Partington. Lucy was a cousin of the writer Martin Amis. She was abducted and murdered. The Wests turned the top floor of their house into a brothel so that Rose could work as a prostitute. Fred West would secretly film her sessions with clients. Fred and Rose were into sadomasochism. They had several more children and continued to kill. The children would later say that they remembered strange incidents where their parents made them hide in a box. It is presumed they did this so the children would not see them disposing of a body.

Fred West's daughter Heather resisted Fred West's sexual advances so she was killed and buried in the garden. In his confession to the police, Fred West complained that Rose West had initially stuffed the body of one of his daughters in a dustbin. He was talking about Heather. In the early 1990s, the social services heard stories about Fred West sexually abusing his daughters so passed the information onto the police. The police arrested Fred and Rose West for the rape of a minor (Rose was charged with assisting the rape). When the police watched the family home videos the Wests had shot of outings to the zoo and parks they noticed that a child seemed to be missing. This was Heather. Fred West said Heather had left home but the police could find no evidence that Heather's national insurance number had been used. She hadn't got a job or claimed any government welfare. She had literally vanished.

The police obtained legal permission to search the house. When the police dug up the West garden and cellar in 1994 they discovered nine bodies. The victims were young women and West children. The bodies at 25 Cromwell Street were buried in the cellar, garden, and under the patio. Fred West was a plasterer by trade - which must have come in handy when he was trying to hide bodies. When the horrors of Cromwell Street were revealed, the neigbours of Fred and

Rose West expressed astonishment that these two seemingly placid people could be capable of murder.

25 Cromwell Street was dubbed the House of Horrors by the British media. Fred West was charged for twelve murders (some murders took place away from Cromwell Street) but hung himself in 1995 before the trial. Fred West hung himself in custody by making a rope from bedsheets he had tied together. He was 53 years-old. Rose West received life in prison at her 1995 trial. The couple had lured young women with the promise of a babysitting job or room to rent and then killed them. The fact they had killed a number of their own children too made the case even more disturbing and unexplainable.

'The revelations during the recent trial of Mrs West (she was found guilty on three counts of murder on November 21, and on a further seven the following day),' wrote one British newspaper, 'were deemed so deeply shocking that even the British gutter press, no enemy to sensation or salaciousness, unanimously declined to print the grimmer details. The jurors were offered psychotherapy after the trial, and some of them may have accepted; the crime reporters present rejected a similar offer with contumely. This solicitousness on the part of the authorities for the emotional welfare of witnesses to the trial was in marked contrast to their previous indifference to the evidence that the Wests were murdering their way through a multitude, almost—but not quite—unmolested for a quarter of a century.'

When the Wests became famous (in the worst possible way), many found it strange to think that Rose West was apparently a sex maniac who not only worked as a prostitute but also helped lure young women into Fred's car. In the 1990s, when the bodies were discovered at Cromwell Street, Rose West was frumpy and overweight with oversized 'granny' specs. However, in the early seventies she was a young woman. She would not have elicited much suspicion back then. One would hardly have looked at the young Rose West and guessed that she was a depraved sexual abuser and psychopath. Fred West might have realised that the game was up in the end but Rose West was in no mood to admit her own guilt. She tried to give the impression that she was merely a victim of Fred West too. To this day she has never admitted any guilt.

Rose West appealed her verdict in 1996 but this was defeated in the courts. She abandoned another appeal in 2001. She seemed to finally accept her fate. However, in 2018 British newspapers reported that Rose West was planning to appeal her case again and still insisted she was innocent. It is of course simply not credible that she lived with Fred West for all those years and had no idea that all these murders were going on. The trial establish that Rose West was a lot more than an innocent bystander. According to research by criminologist Jane Carter Woodrow it was Rose West's insatiable sexual sadism that spurred on the murder spree, with Fred actually following Rose's lead. Rose West is one of only three British women to have ever been handed a full life tariff along with Moors Murderer Myra Hindley and serial killer Joanne Dennhey. She now languishes in prison - where she will surely spend the rest of her life.

(49) DEBRA DENISE BROWN (Years Active 1984, Eight Victims)

Debra Denise Brown was born in 1962. She suffered a head injury as a child and had an exceptionally low IQ. In 1983 she met a man named Alton Coleman and fell under his influence. This was a grim development to say the least because Alton Coleman was a sadistic rapist, killer, and pedophile. Coleman and Brown embarked on a harrowing murder spree in 1984 across several states that often targeted children. Women who are accomplices to male serial killers are sometimes able to put together some sort of case for having been forced and coerced into their activities and in some cases were not actually involved in the actual killing. This was certainly not the case with Debra Denise Brown. She participated in the attacks and sexual assaults and later said she had no regrets and had enjoyed them.

The first victim of this awful duo was nine-year-old Vernita Wheat from Kenosha, Wisconsin. Vernita was raped and then strangled. Nine-year-old Annie and seven-year-old Tamika Turks were the next victims. They were both sexually assaulted in brutal fashion. Annie survived (but was left with terrible injuries as a result of the attack - according to a medical report during the trial her intestines were protruding into her lower region as a result of severe cuts) but Tamika was killed. Coleman and Brown then killed nine-year-old Rachelle Temple in Ohio by strangulation.

This evil duo would also often rob people while on the road - often in violent fashion. The next murder victim was a fifteen year-old girl named Tonnie Storey. By now the activities of Coleman and Brown were starting to attract the attention of the FBI and the police and the net was drawing in. The murderous duo stole a car belonging to Harry Walters (the wife of Harry Walters was raped and beaten to death) and then continued to steal cars and assault people. An elderly man named Eugene Scott was later killed in Indianapolis when the duo stole his car.

Coleman and Brown were arrested three days after their last murder. It was decided to put them on trial in Ohio because that represented the best chance of securing the death penalty. Coleman and Brown were both sentenced to death but in 1991 the death sentence for Brown was commuted to life imprisonment by Ohio Governor Richard Celeste. Celeste was a staunch opponent of capital punishment and argued that Brown, who was deemed to suffer from borderline mental retardation, was manipulated by Coleman.

Alton Coleman was executed though in the end - although it took until 2002 for it to happen. There were so many survivors and relatives of victims that his execution was jam packed and didn't have room for everyone. They had to put it on a closed circuit television feed so everyone could witness it. For those that are curious, for his last meal Coleman chose filet mignon smothered with mushrooms, fried chicken breasts, a salad with French dressing, sweet potato pie topped with whipped cream, French fries, collard greens, onion rings, cornbread, broccoli with melted cheese, biscuits and gravy, and Cherry Coke.

Debra Denise Brown may have been of low intelligence and she may have been dominated by Coleman but she was clearly a sick and evil woman who happily played a full part in these dreadful crimes. She truly did have blood on her hands. In 2005, for the first time, she changed her tune and expressed remorse for her crimes for the first time, apologising to the relatives of the victims. It was all a bit too late for that. Tragically, the damage had already been done.

(48) ELVIRA AND KATE BENDER (Years Active 1871–1872, At Least Eleven Suspected Victims)

The Bloody Benders were a family of serial killers who lived in Labette County, Kansas. From 1871 to 1872 they are believed to have potentially murdered as many as 20 people. They were spiritualists and a German immigrant family. The weird thing about the Bloody Benders is that the mother Elvira and daughter Kate were a full part of the murders. Kate Bender, the daughter, would lure men to their house (which was a sort of general store) and Ma Bender would cook for them. While they were eating, the victims would be hit by a sledgehammer and have their throat cut. The motive for the murders was robbery.

'Homesteaders never really questioned who they were or where they came from,' wrote FilmDaily. 'The family consisted of Ma, Pa, and their two grown children, Kate & John Jr. The family built a one room inn off the Osage Trail so many travelers stopped and frequented their home. They separated the front of the building, which was a store & inn, from the back of the building with a curtain. In the back was their private living quarters. They carried liquor, food, tobacco, horse feed, and gunpowder. Their place was a veritable oasis in the windswept landscape of Cherryvale, Kansas. No one thought anything strange about the Benders until a considerable amount of people started disappearing after staying at their inn.'

The Bloody Benders had their ruse uncovered when they killed a local doctor. The brothers of the doctor organised a huge search for him in the area and the Bender home was searched. It was found to contain bodies which had been sent through a trapdoor. The locals burned down the Bender home. And the Bender family? They had vanished. No one really knows what happened to them. Well, that's more or less how the story goes. One slight problem with the Bloody Benders is that their story has been subject to a certain amount of folklore and embellishment. To this day the true facts of the case and who they were were remain somewhat unverified.

They have though wound their into popular culture and - clearly - the many tales of their grisly exploits from the Old West suggest that this yarn is far from pure myth. The Bloody Benders feel like an obvious inspiration for the crazy Sawyer family in the Texas Chainsaw Massacre films. In 2019 it was reported that 152 acres of land which once belonged to the Bloody Benders had been put up for sale. The strange thing about the report though is that it stated that no excavation of the land had ever taken place - which seems odd given the dark history and lore of the Benders. Who knows what grisly things they might find if they do dig up the site one day.

(47) LOUISE VERMILYA (Years Active 1893–1911, Nine Victims)

Louise Vermilya was born in Cook County, Illinois in 1868. At the age of 16 she married a man named Fred - with whom she lived on near a farm. Fred died at the (then fairly advanced) age of 60 so at the time it wasn't deemed an especially suspicious death at all. He was presumed to have passed away as a consequence of heart trouble. Louise Vermilya received $5,000 as a result of her husband's death as she had made sure he had life insurance. Death though was soon to apparently follow Louise Vermilya around at a rate to rival Charles Bronson in the Death Wish movies.

Not long after Fred died, Vermilya's daughters Cora (who was eight) and Florence (who was four) both passed away. This was followed by the death of Lillian - a 26 year-old granddaughter of Fred. One of the genuinely odd things about Louise Vermilya around this time (and retrospectively it obviously makes more sense) is that the local undertaker later reported that she loved visiting the mortuary. Vermilya wasn't even employed there but she was always trying to find excuses to go to the mortuary and help out. She seemed to get a big kick out of death and being around dead bodies.

Louise got married again - this time to Charles Vermilya. Charles was dead within three years - leaving $1,000 to Louise. The next to bite the bullet was Harry Vermilyea - the step-son of Charles. Harry was said to have had a difficult relationship with Louise Vermilya and they argued a lot. Strangely though, all these deaths of people who had obvious connections to Louise Vermilya had yet to ring any alarm bells or attract any notable degree of scrutiny or suspicion.

In 1910 there was another death in the family when Frank Brinkamp, a son from her marriage to Fred, passed away at the age of 23. Louise Vermilya picked up $1,200 when Frank died. Before he died, Frank told his wife that he was dying in a suspiciously similar fashion to his father. No prizes for guessing who had been killing all of these family members. By now Louise Vermilya had almost run out of relatives to murder and began to target people outside of her family. A man named Jason Ruppert died two days after dining with Louise. The next to die was a man named Richard Smith - who had rented a room from Louise and clearly made the unwitting mistake of eating food prepared by her. He lasted only two days after this fateful meal.

Some reports indicate that Smith married Louise despite the fact he was already married. His other wife expressed some suspicion after learning that her husband had suddenly passed away while with his new flame. Louise Vermilya was finally rumbled when a young police officer named Arthur Bisonette fell ill and died while renting rooms from her. His father had also dined at the house and reported experiencing dreadful stomach pains after the meal. He also recalled that he had seen Louise Vermilya sprinkling a white powder over the food before she served it. A police autopsy on the body of Arthur Bisonette revealed that he had been killed by arsenic. Further exhumations confirmed that Louise Vermilya was a serial poisoner.

There was a bizarre coda to the Louise Vermilya story because she then started poisoning herself in what presumed to be a suicide attempt. She became ill and attended court meetings in a wheelchair. It was then discovered that Arthur Bisonette had been taking a medication that contained traces of arsenic. This made it dificult to convict her for that murder. The prosecution decided to try and convict her on one single charge of murder but they struggled to find enough medical evidence for a 100% cast iron case (despite the fact it was clearly no coincidence that all these people had died around Louise Vermilya).

Further complications ensued from the fact that it was difficult to find an impartial jury because there had been so much press coverage of the case. The prosecution wanted the option of the death penalty but this was impossible because male jurors were not comfortable with sentencing a woman to death - which called into question the likelihood of getting a guilty verdict. In the end the authorities decided a trial would be very expensive and have no guarantee of a conviction so they dropped all the (considerable) charges against Louise

Vermilya and set her free! She didn't last much longer anyway, dying in 1913 at the age of 45. The odd and chilling thing about Louise Vermilya is that while the first murders had a financial motivation the later ones didn't. It seems that she simply enjoyed murdering people.

(46) ANTOINETTE SCIERI (Years Active 1924- 1925, 12+ Victims)

Antoinette Scieri was an Italian woman who moved to France with her family when she was very young. During the First World War she worked at a nursing station which cared for the wounded. Scieri was (like most serial killers it seems) a prolific thief in her early years and stole money and valuables from wounded soldiers. She would even forge letters to their relatives and get them to send her money. As the wounded soldiers were ill or barely awake she was able to get away with her rather heartless thefts and fraud for a time. She was jailed though in 1915 for stealing a soldier's paybook but released after a fairly short sentence.

Scieri got married after this and had some children but the marriage didn't last long and she ended up living with a man named Joseph Rossignol. Joseph Rossignol was a violent drunk and so this relationship was stormy to say the least. In 1920 they moved to the south of France and Antoinette Scieri came up a new way to make money. She got some work caring for elderly people. As you might suspect, having a woman like Antoinette Scieri caring for elderly and vulnerable people was a recipe for disaster. The unfortunate elderly folk under her care soon began shuffling off this mortal coil.

When an elderly husband and wife died while being looked after by Scieri, it roused no suspicion because of their age. It wasn't just her patients who Scieri posed a danger to. She also poisoned her lover Joseph Rossignol to death around this time. Her next victims were two elderly sisters who she poisoned with coffee. One of the sisters found her coffee bitter though and secretly poured it away. The other sister died. This incident fanned the first flames of suspicion concerning Antoinette Scieri.

Her last victim was a woman named Madame Gouan-Criquet. After she died, Gouan-Criquet's husband was very suspicious of the fact that his wife's condition seemed to get markedly worse each time she was visited by Antoinette Scieri. When he looked under the bed of his wife he found a bottle of the herbicide pyralion. Antoinette Scieri had finally been rumbled. The bodies of a number of people who had died after being 'cared' for by Scieri were exhumed and found to contain pyralion. These of course included the body of Joseph Rossignol.

Antoinette Scieri tried to pretend she was innocent and blamed the murders on a neighbour but this was all nonsense. She eventually confessed and was sentenced to death in 1926. The death sentence though was commuted to life in prison and she died behind bars. Antoinette Scieri was a classic example of a killer who dons the 'mask of sanity' and hides in plain sight. She was said to have an excellent bedside manner and those people who employed her thought she was kind and caring. Nothing could be further from the real truth. The authorities deemed her to be of sound mind and not insane. She knew exactly what she was doing and was a calm and calculating killer.

(45) TILLIE KLIMEK (Years Active 1914-1921, Suspected of 10+ Murders)

Ottilie 'Tillie' Klimek was born Teofila Gburek on October the 22nd, 1877 in Poland. Her family moved to the United States when she was an infant. In 1914 she got married and her husband died in 1914 after a sudden illness. Her second husband died soon after - as a did a lover who had given her the elbow. Tillie's third husband was a man named Frank Kupczyk. Frank died in 1921. The odd and suspicious thing about this death at the time was that Tillie seemed to anticipate it as going to happen. Legend has it that Tillie even purchased a coffin before Frank had passed away.

Husband number four for Tillie was Joseph Klimek. However, when Klimek fell ill the doctors who treated him became suspicious and decided to run some tests. Sure enough, the medical findings reported arsenic poisoning. Tillie's cousin Nellie Koulik was also arrested because she was alleged to have supplied the poison and been an accomplice. Exhumations confirmed that Tille's previous husbands had all been poisoned. The investigation which followed discovered that neighbours and other relatives of Tillie had fallen ill or died after consuming food or drinks prepared by her.

Tillie was sentenced to life in prison while Nellie got a year behind bars. Tillie died in 1936 at the age of 60. The media at the time reported that Tillie was a psychic who predicted when her victims were going to die. This wasn't really true and more of a speculative embellishment than anything. It was probably a result of Tillie buying a coffin for her husband Frank before he died. This was hardly evidence of being a psychic. She had poisoned him so she knew full well he was going to die soon!

We don't know how many people Tillie Klimek killed for sure. Although she was only convicted of one murder, prosecutors at the trial apparently amassed enough evidence to plausibly connect Tillie to twenty suspicious deaths. Tillie Klimek made no effort to feign innocence or deny that she'd killed anyone. When asked if she'd murdered members of family at the trial she simply shrugged and admitted it as if it was all no big deal. The motivation for the murders is believed to have been (no surprise here) money. Tillie always tried to make sure her husbands had life insurance policies before she slipped them the dreaded arsenic.

(44) DOROTHEA PUENTE (Years Active 1982–1988, Nine Verified Victims, Several

Other Suspected Victims)

Dorothea Puente was born Dorothea Helen Gray in 1929 in Redlands, California. She tends to be known as The Death House Landlady in true crime lore. Her childhood was absolutely awful. Her parents were alcoholics and she ended up in an orphanage where she suffered from sexual abuse. She was married in 1945 and had two children but the marriage didn't last for long and she sent the children away to live with relatives or be adopted. She also suffered a miscarriage.

In 1948, Dorothea Puente served a few months in jail for using bogus cheques. She got married again in 1952 but this was an obstreperous affair by all accounts. Puente was never faithful to her husband and alleged to fritter money away gambling. Puente went from fraud to prostitution in the years that followed and ended up running a brothel. In 1960 she was arrested for this and served another short prison sentence. In 1968, she married Roberto Jose Puente - from whom she got her infamous surname. Puente was much younger than his wife and the marriage only lasted sixteen months. He fled back to Mexico in the end.

Dorothea Puente switched careers again at this point and became a nurse's assistant. She eventually began managing boarding houses. Dorothea Puente ran a boarding house in Sacramento that housed elderly and mentally handicapped boarders. Puente was considered to be a pillar of the community and greatly respected. She looked like Grandma Walton and seemed to be the least threatening and most caring person imaginable. Nothing could be further from the actual truth though. Puente was responsible for cashing the social security cheques of her vulnerable tenants. Given her history of fraud this was a classic case of letting the fox run free in the hen house.

In 1978, Dorothea Puente was found guilty of cashing dozens of federal cheques that belonged to her tenants. However, she simply had to pay costs and go on probation. She was soon back to her old ways - only this time in more deadly fashion. Puente began to kill her boarders with drugs and then continue to cash their cheques after they had died. Because many of the boarders had no family she was able to get away with this for a time. She is believed to have made around $5000 a month from this scheme.

Ruth Monroe was Puente's first known murder victim. Monroe and Puente were actually business partners. Puente killed her with an overdose of codeine and Tyleno and then inherited a large sum of money from the estate of the victim. Some of Puente's victims were suffocated with a pillow. She put the body of one victim in a coffin and left it on a riverbank. Some of the victims were buried in Puente's basement. Neighbours sometimes detected a strange and pungent smell - which they complained about but obviously did not deduce was the result of dead bodies. You can hardly blame them. Who could have guessed that this seemingly sweet old lady was bumping off her boarders?

One victim even had the head and hands removed to lessen the chances of identification. The head and hands of this victim were never found. On investigating the disappearance of a man named Alberto Montoya, the police went to speak to Puente and noticed some loose soil on her property. No prizes for guessing why this soil was loose. Bodies were soon discovered. Amazingly, Puente wasn't a suspect at first and had been given permission by the police to go and get some coffee. She fled and booked into a hotel in Los Angeles under an assumed name. Puente was thankfully captured though and brought back to Sacramento to stand trial.

It took five years for the trial to take place - by which time Puente was 64 years-old. Puente's defence team tried to argue that she was simply a thief and fraudster who had never killed anyone. The prosecution and - crucially - the evidence said otherwise. They proved that a sedative named Dalmane had been found in several of the victims. It was even argued at the trial that Puente had paid former convicts to help her dispose of the bodies. Puente was charged with three counts of murder and sentenced to life in prison. She died in 2011 at the age of 82 and never confessed to her crimes.

(43) TAMARA IVANYUTINA (Years Active 1976–1987, At Least Nine Victims)

Tamara Ivanyutina was born in the Ukrainian SSR in 1841. Ivanyutina has a small if rather unwelcome place in history as she was the last woman to be executed in the Soviet Union. The pretty odd thing about Tamara Ivanyutina is that most of her family seemed to be serial killers. If you got on the wrong side of them they would simply slip some thallium into your food and drink. Tamara's parents are said to have once poisoned a cousin for the high crime of spreading some idle gossip about them.

The family as a collective are said to have poisoned over forty people and around thirteen of these incidents turned out to be fatal. As for Tamara alone, she is generally credited with nine solo murders. She killed her first husband so she could have his apartment and when she got married again she killed her father-in-law because she wanted his house. Poisoning was considered to be something of a must have skill in the Ivanyutina family. Tamara even tutored her sister Nina in the art of poisoning because her sister had an annoying husband she wanted to bump off.

In the mid 1980s, Tamara got a job as a dishwasher in a school in the Podolsk district of Kiev. As you might fear and expect, a prolific and compulsive poisoner like Tamara Ivanyutina working in a school was never going to have much of a happy ending. In 1987, staff and pupils at the school where Tamara worked began to mysteriously fall ill. Two children and two adults died very quickly. The dietitian at the school had been poisoned a few weeks before. It came as no surprise to later learn that Tamara Ivanyutina was said to loathe this dietitian because she was snooty and rude to humble dishwashers.

An investigation into the deaths and illnesses at the school looked into the food because the survivors were now in hospital with severe stomach problems. The police also exhumed the body of the dietitian who had died and found traces of thallium. The investigation now drew up a list of all staff at the school who had access to the kitchen. Tamara Ivanyutina was on that list and had her house searched where - sure enough - investigators found a bottle of poison that matched the poison found in the victim. She was arrested and found to have got the job in the school with fake ID (that hid her past criminal convictions).

The investigation further revealed that the Ivanyutina family procured poison from the Geological Institute and that most of the family had killed people. Tamara's sister got fifteen years, her father and mother – respectively ten and thirteen years. Tamara was sentenced to death and executed in 1987. The family tried to bribe the authorities into letting them off but that obviously didn't work. Tamara was very reluctant to offer any confessions but she did seem to imply that she poisoned the children because they always irritated her by not stacking the chairs correctly in the canteen after lunch. Let that be a lesson to all schoolchildren. Stack those chairs tidily because you never know who might be working in the kitchen!

(42) JEANNE WEBER (Years Active 1905-1908, Seven Victims)

Jeanne Weber was born in France in 1875. Weber tends to be known as The Ogress of the Goutte-d'Or Street in true crime lore. She moved to Paris and got married as a young women but her husband left - leaving her with three children. In the community in which she lived Jeanne Weber was well liked and respected and seemed to be a kind, friendly woman to all who met her. It came as no surprise then that she was frequently asked to be a babysitter for local children and relatives. In 1905 she was asked to look after her brother's two-year daughter Georgette but tragedy struck when Georgette died. The death was not deemed to be suspicious but the truth was chilling. Jeanne Weber had strangled Georgette.

A few days later there was another death in the family when two year-old Suzanne, another niece, died while being looked after by Jeanne Weber. The death was recorded as a case of respiratory malfunction. Jeanne Weber wasn't suspected at all because the thought that she could harm her brother's children was so preposterous no one even dreamed of it. Weber killed her last remaining niece Germaine only days later in similar circumstances. This time the death was written off as diphtheria (an infection caused by strains of bacteria called Corynebacterium diphtheriae that make toxin).

Only four days later, Jeanne Weber's son Marcel was dead. It was later established that these children all had marks on their necks and throats when they died. It is strange indeed then that no one seemed to detect anything suspicious about the tragedies. Despite all of these cases, Weber's sister-in-law asked her to look after her ten year-old son Maurice while she went out shopping with a friend. When she returned from her shopping trip she found Maurice gasping for breath with Jeanne Weber astride him. Weber was said to have had a deranged look on her face as if she was completely crazy. No surprise there as she clearly WAS completely crazy. Maurice died a few hours later in hospital and Jeanne Weber was arrested.

It then came to light that two other children in the family had previously passed away suddenly in somewhat mysterious circumstances. Weber was put on trial for seven murders. Her lawyer, believe it or not, argued that she didn't murder anyone and was simply unlucky to have been there when all these children dropped dead of natural causes. That was an interesting and rather ludicrous defence. Astonishingly though, Weber was actually cleared of all charges because - despite exhumations - they couldn't establish enough medical evidence against her.

Jeanne Weber, now calling herself Jeanne Glaize, then moved to a village where she got a position with a man named Sylvain Bavouzet. Weber's duties? Well, she was hired to look Bavouzet's children. Inevitably, tragedy soon struck the Bavouzet family when nine year-old Auguste was found dead. He had a mark around his neck that was (wrongly) presumed to have been a consequence of his tight clothes. There was a fortunate development next though when Germaine, the oldest of the children at sixteen, found an old article about the dreaded Ogress of the Goutte-d'Or Street. The family quickly deduced that Jeanne Glaize was actually the notorious Jeanne Weber.

However, yet again, Weber somehow got away with her crimes. The death of Auguste was judged to be a result of typhoid fever and Weber was released. Jeanne Weber now changed her name to Marie Lamoine and promptly got a job in a (yes, you guessed it) orphanage. It didn't take too long at all for her to be caught in the act of trying to strangle a child. The owners of the orphanage decided not to take action because they thought it would be bad for business so they simply fired Weber and told her to sling her hook.

Jeanne Weber ended up back in Paris where she turned to prostitution and got married to a criminal. Her activities as a serial strangler finally came to an end when she was caught trying to strangle the son of a hostel owner. After this latest arrest she finally confessed to her crimes and was banished to a mental hospital. After ten years in captivity she committed suicide in 1918 at the age of 43.

(41) ENRIQUETA MARTI RIPOLLES (Years Active 1902-1912, 10+ Alleged Victims)

Enriqueta Martí was born in Catalonia in 1868. As a young woman she moved to Barcelona and became a prostitute. She is said to have got married but this was apparently a stormy affair that didn't last very long. Enriqueta Martí opened her own brothel but found that some of the clients there had particular (not to mention criminal) tastes and liked young children. Enriqueta Martí therefore began abducting children so she could 'pimp' them in her brothel to paedophiles.

As if that wasn't bad enough, Martí was also killing them to make all manner of creams and potions in her self-styled role as a mystical guru and witch-doctor. Enriqueta Martí is even said to have drank the blood of her child victims because she believed drinking blood cured medical ailments and kept one healthy. Martí was arrested in 1909 when it came to light she used children in her brothel but she escaped any serious charges and was not punished for these crimes. It is assumed that because some police officers used the brothel, Martí was able to use this information to get herself off the hook.

Her activities, all told, went on for some time and more children were inevitably abducted after her close brush with the law. She was finally arrested in 1912. It is claimed she was caught when a little girl at the brothel went to a window and was seen by someone outside. Enriqueta Martí always told the abducted children to stay away from the windows. The police found two little girls in the brothel and Enriqueta Martí (rather unconvincingly) told them that one girl was her daughter and another was an orphan she was looking after.

'The girls told the police that their captor would only feed them potatoes and bread,' wrote STSTW Media. 'She would pinch them if they misbehaved such as going to the windows, balconies or other rooms. Those other rooms told a story even darker than kidnapping. The girls were first to explore them in their bored isolation beforehand and so guided the police inside. There they found bloody clothes and a myriad of evidence to incarcerate the supposed vampiress. Thirty small bones, many of which exposed to fire was one such proof. There were many jars with strange remains, blood, bones and hair. There were clothes covered in blood, knives and bones.

Angelita also spoke of a young boy called Pepito who she witnessed being killed by a knife on the kitchen table by Martí.'

The police are said to have found hidden walls in the brothel which contained the grisly potions (said to be popular with the elites of Barcelona because Enriqueta Martí told them they cured tuberculosis) and alleged human bones. Enriqueta Martí didn't really offer a confession in the end. She said she was responsible for the unusual potions but never admitted to killing anyone. She also refused to reveal the names of clients who used her brothel and purchased her potions. Enriqueta Martí was never actually tried in the end. She was taken into custody and died just over a year later when other prisoners beat her to death. Martí is naturally known as The Vampire of Barcelona in crime articles today.

The story of Enriqueta Martí is strange and grisly indeed but not believed by everyone. Some writers believe she was made a scapegoat for the fact that the police were struggling to solve a rash of child abductions in the area. There appears to be enough evidence though to suggest that, at the very least, Enriqueta Martí was a sinister and dangerous character with a rather dodgy and wayward moral compass.

(40) NANNIE DOSS (Years Active 1927–1954, Eleven Verified Victims)

Nannie Doss was born in Blue Mountain, Alabama, in 1905. Here is one of the most unlikely serial killers on our list. Nannie Doss was a benign looking grandmother who killed eleven relatives before her crimes were uncovered. She is forever known in true crime circles as The Giggling Granny. She showed no remorse at her crimes and even seemed amused whenever she had to reflect on them. The story of Nannie Doss began with her working on a farm as a child. This wasn't much of a life and she hated it. She wasn't in school much thanks to her farm duties and so was never the most intelligent person. She got married at sixteen and had four children - two of whom died. This first marriage didn't last long. Nannie's husband seemed to despise her and was never at home. She was said to drink a lot to curb her loneliness.

Her second marriage was more enduring. Doss spent sixteen years with her second husband and gained some grandchildren over this period. However, two of these grandchilden died while in the custody of Nannie Doss. This same year, Nannie's husband also died. The culprit in these suspicious deaths was Nannie Doss. Nannie's daughter was very suspicious of her mother because she noticed that Nannie had a bizarre habit of sticking pins in the grandchildren when no one was looking. Nannie's husband was a victim of rat poison. Nannie would usually put the poison in cakes she had baked and then serve it up to the victim - in this case her husband. However, the authorities treated none of these deaths as suspicious.

The deadly deeds of Nannie Doss were not over yet. She married for a third time but her new husband didn't last very long. He was presumed to have died of a heart attack but that doesn't seem very likely with Nannie Doss around. Nannie then burnt their house down so that she would be entitled to insurance money. Nannie married again and quickly dispatched her latest husband with rat poison. She then murdered her mother.

In 1953, Nannie found another husband and poisoned him to get her hands on the life insurance polices in his name. This time though her luck finally ran out. When the authorities (not before time you might suggest!) became suspicious of yet another death connected to Nannie Doss, a medical examination found huge amounts of arsenic in the body of her latest late husband. Nannie Doss was arrested and confessed to all the murders. She giggled when she made her confession and seemed completely relaxed and calm talking about her crimes. Nannie Doss seemed to actually enjoy talking about the murders she had committed and acted as if it had all been great fun.

The only possible explanation for Nannie Doss is that as a child she apparently suffered a bad head injury when she was hit with a metal bar (that came off a train). It seems plausible that this left her with some sort of mental impairment. She was clearly not a sane or normal woman. A surprisingly high number of serial killers received head injuries from an accident when still a child. There is a theory that this impairs the part of the brain responsible for ruminating on the consequences of one's actions.

Nannie Doss was sentenced to life in prison at her trial. Her gender is probably the only thing that saved her from the death penalty. She died in the Oklahoma State Penitentiary in 1965 at the age of 59. It is said that her last husband was found with enough arsenic in him to kill a horse. Nannie Doss liked to put arsenic in cakes but she also laced moonshine with poison and gave it to her husbands. When she was in custody she denied that her motivation for the murders had been financial. Nannie Doss said she was simply looking for the perfect husband. "I was searching for the perfect mate," she said, by way of explanation for why she kept bumping of husbands. "The real romance of life."

(39) LAINZ ANGELS OF DEATH (Years Active 1983-1989, 40+ Suspected Victims)

The Lainz Angels of Death were Maria Gruber, Irene Leidolf, Stephanija Meyer, and Waltraud Wagner. This quartet were Austrian nurses who murdered dozens of patients at a Vienna hospital by giving them overdoses of morphine or putting water into their lungs. Waltraud Wagner was the first of the women to kill but they all conspired and worked together in the end when it came to killing patients.

Three of the women were very young (Maria Gruber in particular was only a teenager) but Stephanija Meyer was in her forties and her age made her the most charismatic of the group. She arguably wielded the most influence. The nurses would pinch the nose of victims and pour water in them. Many of these patients were very feeble and unable to struggle. Few of these patients were terminally ill and they would have lived to leave hospital were it not for these evil women.

Waltraud Wagner, who recruited the other nurses into this heartless activity, had classic symptoms of God complex - a familiar trait of serial killers who work in the medical profession. Wagner loved the sense of power she had over these patients and clearly enjoyed taking lives. The Lainz Angels of Death were captured when they were overheard bragging about their murders in a pub. They were thankfully taken into custody very quickly.

It later transpired that investigators had raised alarm bells about a suspicious death at the hospital in 1988 but couldn't go very far in their investigation because of the lack of cooperation from the hospital (who clearly wanted to brush the suspicious death under the carpet lest there be any legal complications). The women confessed to over forty murders but the true figure is impossible to say. Some accounts of this case they might have potentially killed over a hundred people.

Wagner was convicted of 15 murders, 17 attempts, and two counts of assault. She was sentenced to life in prison. Irene Leidolf also received a life sentence for five murders. Wagner and Leidolf tried to claim the murders had been mercy killings of terminally ill patients but this simply didn't wash when subjected to sustained scrutiny in court. Meyer and Gruber received twenty years in prison for manslaughter and attempted murder. Meyer and Gruber were released fairly soon and given new identities. That was surprising but even more controversial was the release of Wagner and Leidolf in 2008 for 'good behaviour' in prison.

The preposterously early release of these women caused outrage in Austria and made both the media and public alike wonder if the country's justice system was too soft and forgiving. It hardly must have seemed fair to the relatives of the victims that these four awful women had barely spent any time in prison at all for their dreadful and chilling crimes. It is amazing really to think that they were all released from prison so soon - as if their crimes had been petty or not that serious. Off the top of my head I can't think of many more serious crimes than murdering helpless patients in a hospital.

(38) MADAME DE BRINVILLIERS (Years Active 1666-1670, Three Victims, Dozens of Alleged Other Victims)

Marie-Madeleine d'Aubray - Marquise de Brinvilliers was born in Paris in 1630. She was a French aristocrat who murdered her father and brothers in order to inherit their estates. However, it is often claimed that killed dozens of people in hospitals while testing and refining the poison which she would used to kill her relatives. The truth of this later claim is disputed but it wouldn't surprise you if it was true. Marquise de Brinvilliers was clearly a ruthless and ambitious woman who would stop at nothing to get what she wanted. You can't imagine she was the sort of person who would lose much sleep over some people in hospital getting poisoned!

The Marquise was the eldest of the children in her family but she was not in line to inherit the estate. As a woman she was expected to marry into wealth and not burden the family. She had marriages and children but the Marquise was very promiscuous and had many lovers. This is said to have rankled her father because he felt she was risking shame on the family reputation. The Marquise's father was very angry when he learned that his daughter was having an affair with a man named Godin de Sainte-Croix so he arranged for Sainte-Croix to be arrested. It is naturally speculated that this action made the Marquise angry enough to contemplate murdering her father.

Godin de Sainte-Croix started an alchemy business when he was released from prison. He remained in (clandestine you would imagine) contact with the Marquise and through Sainte-Croix she learned a great deal about chemicals and poisons. It is claimed that the Marquise now conducted a number of experiments with poison on a local hospital in Paris and also on her own servants. Up to thirty people are alleged to have died as a result of these experiments. The source for this claim is a police report although, as we have noted, not everyone believes this happened. One can certainly build a case for it though.

Noble French figures were often expected to visit hospitals and the Marquise would have had ample opportunity to poison patients. Suspicious deaths in hospitals at the time would hardly have been noticed or logged in the 1660s in the way they would today. People simply died a lot more often in those days than they do today. Medical treatment was primitive and disease was more rampant. The Marquise could have offed a number of patients and servants for all we know.

In 1666 she began to poison her father. The Marquise actually put an employee of hers in the family home to finish her father off with poison. Her father, shortly before his death, invited her home and so she actually finished him off herself in the end. The Marquise then set about poisoning her brothers. This was a lot more difficult because she wasn't on good terms with them and they barely spoke to her. They did though live in the family home so she got a footman employed by the family to help her. One of the brothers was poisoned with an apple pie and they managed to get to the other brother too in the end.

Strangely, the Marquise seemed to get away with the murders at first despite the fact that they were highly suspicious. She was rumbled though when Godin de Sainte-Croix died. He was found to have letters in his possession from the Marquise in which she'd promised him a sum of money after the deaths of her father and brothers had been completed. Case closed. The participation of La Chaussée, the footman who helped in the murders, was also deduced and he fled. When he was captured, La Chaussée admitted that the Marquise had been behind the deaths of her relatives. The Marquise went on the run and tried to hide in England. She was eventually arrested in Belgium.

The Marquise at first denied all knowledge of the murders and said she had nothing to do with them. She said that Godin de Sainte-Croix must have killed them. However, she was not believed and sentenced to death. The Marquise was subject to a torture known as water cure before her death. In this rather unpleasant practice the victim is forced to drink large quantities of water in a short time until their stomach is full and they can barely breathe. The Marquise was then beheaded with a sword in 1676. She was 45 years-old.

(37) GESCHE GOTTFRIED (Years Active 1813-1827, Fifteen Victims)

Gesche Gottfried was born born Gesche Margarethe Timm in Germany in 1831. She was known as The Angel of Bremen and poisoned fifteen people to death. It made no difference to Gottfried who the person was. She happily poisoned friends and relatives. Gesche Gottfried grew up in a large and poor family and always felt rather unloved. It is speculated that she later developed Munchausen syndrome by proxy (MSP). In medical terms, this is defined as a disorder in which the caretaker of a person either makes up fake symptoms or causes real symptoms to make it appear as though the person is injured or ill. The term by proxy means through a substitute.

Though MSP is primarily a mental illness, it is also considered a form of abuse. Many people with MSP exaggerate or lie about a person's symptoms to get attention. They may also create symptoms by poisoning food, withholding food, or causing an infection. Some people may even have a person undergo painful or risky tests and procedures to try to gain sympathy from their family members or community.

Gesche Gottfried poisoned to death, among others, two husbands, her mother and father, two daughters and a son, her brother, a fiancé, and numerous friends. She enjoyed the sympathy that people gave her as a result of these deaths. They obviously had no idea that Gottfried was killing these people so showered her with sympathy and support each time she 'suffered' the loss of a presumed loved one. She would mix rat poison in animal fat and then slip this into the food of her victims. She often killed people slowly by giving them small amounts of poison at a time. Once the victim started to become ill, Gottfriend would of course volunteer to care for them.

Part of the motivation for these murders was obviously money as Gesche collected a number of inheritances as a result of so many relatives dying. She was creative with her methods and once poisoned someone through a dish of shellfish. Her exploits came to an end when one would be victim noticed some white power on food that Gesche had given him. He consulted a local doctor about this and the substance was identified as arsenic. Gesche was arrested in 1828. She was 43 years-old at the time. Gesche Gottfried was sentenced to death by decapitation and beheaded on April the 21st 1831. This was the last public execution ever carried out in the city of Bremen.

(36) MARIE ALEXANDER BECKER (Years Active 1933–1936, Eleven Victims)

Marie Alexandrine Becker was born in 1877 in Waasmont, Landen, Belgium. When she was a young woman she got a job in a sewing shop and began what seemed to be a happy and successful life. She eventually worked at a large fashion store on Pot d'Or Street in Liège and in 1906 married a man named Charles Becker Sr who had two sons. Behind the scenes though she wasn't happy. She found her husband dull and bickered with his relatives.

Marie eventually began to feel that life had passed her by and decided she wanted to make up for lost time. She eventually began an affair with a man named Lambert Beyer and poisoned her husband with digitalis (a drug used for heart diseases). She then poisoned her lover too. Marie was clearly having something of a mid-life crisis because she took to visiting nightclubs and gathered a collection of young lovers (most of whom she had to bribe to share her bed). This all cost money and so she boosted her income by murdering the elderly patrons of her dress shop. She would slip the poison in a cup of tea and then when it began to take effect would take the victim home so they died in their house rather than her shop. This obviously made the deaths far less suspicious.

Marie is thought to have carried out at least eleven murders but many crime experts believe she probably murdered more people than this. She was a financially motivated serial killer. Marie simply wanted money to maintain her lifestyle and was perfectly willing to kill people if that was the only way to do this. She would only manage though to get hold of a minor sum of money from each victim. It wasn't exactly a rapid get rich scheme. Marie would even attend the funerals of many of her victims and was a convincing actress by all accounts, seeming suitably distraught at the gravesite.

However, once the funeral was over Becker would soon be back in a bar or nightclub seeming as if she didn't have a care in the world. She would mock her victims and make jokes about them in private. Marie Alexandrine Becker was not someone who was ever burdened by human emotions like guilt or remorse. Her killing spree came to an end when one of Marie's friends told her she was in an unhappy marriage. Marie told her friend that she should poison her husband and offered to supply the poison. The friend was rather disturbed by this and went to the police.

Marie Alexandrine Becker was found to have in her possession a bottle of poison and clothes and jewelry belonging to her elderly victims. Exhumations confirmed that a number of victims had died by poisoning. Marie insisted she was innocent and said the digitalis was for personal use but this was all complete nonsense. There was simply too much evidence against her. She was found guilty of eleven murders, five attempted murders, theft and forgery. The sentence was execution but this was commuted to life in prison. Marie Alexandrine Becker died in prison in Nazi occupied Belgium in 1942. She was 62 years old.

(35) CLEMENTINE BARNABET (Years Active 1911–1912, Seventeen Suspected Victims)

Clementine Barnabet was born in St. Martinville, Louisiana in 1894. Banabet was supposedly the priestress of a cult group called The Church of Sacrifice. You can probably guess what this nutty cult group believed in. The clue is in the title. Her family moved to Lafayette around the turn of the century and were all involved in this cult. In 1911, led by Clementine, the cult slaughtered some families by barging into their homes. The method of murder was an axe - which naturally made these killings incredibly brutal and bloody. The axe murders then seemed to move to Texas - which somewhat puzzled the authorities. They genuinely had no idea what the motive for these axe slayings was. It didn't seem to be financial or sexual.

The breakthrough came when the mistress of Clementine's brother Raymond told the police that he was part of a cult who were killing people with axes. Raymond was arrested and put in prison but the murders continued. The police decided to visit the home of Raymond's family and found that Clementine was in possession of blood splattered clothes. She was arrested along with three other cult members. Clementine confessed to seventeen murders. She told the police that her cult group believed in human sacrifice as it was the path to immortality. Unbelievably, she was deemed sane and released from prison five years later for good behaviour! Several years later, a killer known as The Axeman of New Orleans murdered six people in similar fashion to the modus operandi of the Sacrifice cult. The

Axeman (or woman?) was never captured. Clementine could never be found either. No one knows what happened to her or where she went.

(34) ROBERTA ELDER (Years Active 1938-1952, 14+ Suspected Victims)

Roberta Elder was a Georgia serial killer who is believed to have poisoned at least fourteen people. She is believed to have killed for the first time in 1938. Her first victim was her husband John Woodward. Six months later, Roberta Elder's son from a previous also died at the age of thirteen. The victim count escalated from here on in. Elder killed more husbands, more children, and even a grandchild. It was only in 1952 that anyone began to suspect that something was suspicious about this family.

Rev. William H. Elder, who was the latest husband of Roberta Elder, fell ill after eating his packed lunch on a construction site. The doctor was called for and he had time to examine Rev. William H. Elder before the man passed away from what seemed to be a severe stomach complaint. The doctor became suspicious because the reddish tinge in the skin of the dying victim reminded him of a tinge in the skin of two Elder family children who had previously passed away. The doctor decided to bring in a coroner - who decided to do a test for arsenic. When this proved positive, exhumations on deceased Elder relatives took place and also found evidence of arsenic. It probably didn't come as a huge shock to learn that Roberta Elder was the financial beneficiary of these deaths when it came to life insurance.

It later transpired that were cases of Roberta arranging life insurance on relatives only weeks before they died. Like other notorious poisoners, Roberta Elder always made sure that she was the one tasked with looking after a family member when they fell ill. Roberta was arrested on suspicion of murder. She ludicrously claimed that she'd never heard of arsenic and knew nothing about poisoning but this was clearly not the case. Indeed, it was later established that she got hold of the poison from her brother's farm. Roberta Elder was found guilty of murder and sentenced to life in prison. She had literally killed everyone in her family.

No one was safe from Roberta Elder. She even killed little kids. And yet, despite her crimes there is very little information about Roberta Elder and her exploits. She is far less famous than other female serial killers (even ones who killed less people). This is felt to be because Roberta Elder was black and her victims were black. At the time this case was not deemed worthy of as much ink as a case involving white victims would receive. Sad but true, it seems that this case would be much more famous today if Elder and her victims had been white.

'Though Roberta Elder's victims died decades ago,' wrote aaihs.org, 'the phenomenon of consistently devaluing Black violent crime victims remains to this day, evidenced by the persistent public fascination with Nannie Doss and her white victims, while Roberta Elder and the victims she is accused of killing remain forgotten. Between 1952 and 1954, the Black press followed Elder's case through the criminal justice system, while law enforcement found more potential victims to blame on Elder and the white press took little interest. Meanwhile, mainstream media became distracted by the Giggling Granny who continues to attract infamy as a notorious female serial killer. The danger in ignoring Black victims is not only in the devaluation of Black life, but also in ignoring systemic oppression that makes Black people more vulnerable to violent crime and less likely to receive justice.'

(33) GUADALUPE MARTINEZ DE BEJARANO (Years Active 1887–1892, Three Victims)

Guadalupe Martínez de Bejarano is often called Mexico's first female serial killer and is known as La Mujer Verdugo (The Executioner Woman). The life of Guadalupe Martínez de

Bejarano before her crimes is rather vague and nothing much is known about her childhood and birth. We do know though that she got married at some point and had a child. Martínez would find victims by interviewing people in her home with a view to employing them as a servant. This was all a ruse though. She would instead enslave and torture them.

Martínez was a sadist with a sexual motivation for her crimes. It is often assumed that only male serial killers are motivated by sexual desires but women like Guadalupe Martínez de Bejarano illustrate that this is not the case at all. The victims were lulled into a false sense of security because Martínez seemed fairly normal at first glance and had quite a middle-class sort of background. Being trapped in the home of Martínez turned out to be a nightmare. Once she had restrained her victims she would sexually abuse them and whip them ferociously. Some were hung from the ceiling or burnt. The victims were all female so we can safely presume that Martínez was probably a closet lesbian.

Martínez would starve the victims after she had satiated her sick and sadistic desires. The first victim was a girl named Casimira Juárez in 1887. Martínez was actually convicted for this murder but (unbelievably) only served a few years in prison. Her next victims were two sisters named Guadalupe and Crescencia Pineda in 1892. Neighbours of Martínez had by now started to notice that something strange was going on. There were a lot of dark whispers about her. The police took action after hearing these complaints and found the dead bodies of the Pineda sisters.

Martínez tried to blame the murders on her son Aurelio and said she was completely innocent. However, her son told the police that his mother was a kidnapper, sadist, and murderer who had carried out these murders herself. This did rather beg the question of why Aurelio hadn't saved the victims or told the police about his mother before now. As a consequence, although he had nothing to do with the murders, Aurelio received a prison sentence for not doing anything to stop them nor report his mother to the police.

As for Guadalupe Martínez de Bejarano, for the crime of torturing and murdering three young women, she was sentenced to ten years in prison. It felt like a ludicrously light sentence given the gravity of the crimes and there was much outrage in Mexico that she didn't get the death penalty. It was all moot in the end though as Guadalupe Martínez de Bejarano died in prison fairly soon into her sentence. One might say that prison was a worse punishment than the death penalty for Guadalupe Martínez de Bejarano because she had a pretty rough time in prison and was under constant threat of attack from other inmates because of the cruel and disturbing nature of her crimes.

(32) LINDA HAZZARD (Years Active 1911, Fifteen+ Victims)

Linda Hazzard was born in 1867 in Carver, Minnesota. Hazzard was one of eight children and seems to have had a fairly normal background. Around 1904, she met a man named Samuel Christman Hazzard. Samuel was a thief and conman who had been kicked out of the army for stealing. He married Linda but because he was already married he served a prison sentence for bigamy. After his release from prison he moved to Washington with Linda Hazzard. Linda Hazzard obtained a medical licence issued by the state of Washington thanks to a loophole. This meant she could now call herself Dr Linda Hazzard. There was only one problem. Hazzard had no medical training and no medical degree. She was what is known in the trade as a quack doctor.

You might say that Hazzard was ahead of her time when it came to alternative medicine but that would be an insult to alternative medicine. Hazzard's own brand of treatment was downright criminal. Hazzard opened the sanitarium Wilderness Heights in Olalla, Washington. She believed that the key to health was fasting and had even published three books about this. 'Appetite is Craving,' she wrote. 'Hunger is Desire. Craving is never satisfied; but Desire is relieved when Want is supplied.' At her sanitarium, patients were literally starved to death. Hazzard insisted that the best way to remove toxins from the body was to abstain from food as much as possible. So, if you checked into her sanitarium your typical day's food would sometimes be a single orange or perhaps a few sips of broth.

Linda Hazzard was a remarkably persuasive woman though because she persuaded any number of ordinary rational people that this crackpot treatment was for the best. Patients were often treated at her house first and then moved to this dubious 'sanitarium' when they got weak and sick from the lack of food. The patients were usually from quite well heeled families (you might say there is no fool like a rich fool!) and in addition to being starved they also had to endure daily enemas. It's amazing really that anyone was willing to put up with this.

In 1908 two patients died as a result of the extreme fasting treatment of Linda Hazzard. In 1909 two more patients died. The local health authorities, strangely, did not take any action though because they argued that the patients had submitted to this treatment voluntarily. Linda Hazzard said that the patients had died as a result of medical conditions they already had and that her methods had nothing to do with the deaths. That was plainly nonsense. There was a curious incident this same year when a young man from New Zealand was found dead on the property from a gunshot wound. The young man was related to British nobility and not short of money. It is naturally presumed then that Samuel and Linda might have had a hand in his death for financial reasons.

There were more deaths in the next two years that followed. Healthy people who weren't even old were ruined by this starvation diet and became emaciated skeletons who could barely get out of bed. The two most famous victims were British sisters Claire and Dorothea Williamson. Once Linda Hazzard deduced that these two sisters were wealthy she transferred them to her home where they were put on a diet of tomato broth and nothing else. Margaret Conway, the childhood nanny of the sisters, then arrived to visit them. She was shocked by what she discovered. Claire was dead and Dora weighed 50 pounds and was at death's door.

Conway then discovered that Claire had left her estate to Linda Hazzard before she died and that Hazzard had also appointed herself the legal guardian of Dorothea. Hazzard had also been helping herself to the clothes and jewelry owned by the sisters. With the help of Dorothea's uncle, Conway managed to get Dorothea out of the house and rescue her. Linda Hazzard then actually had the nerve to ask for a £2,000 fee for the treatment the sisters had received!

Dorothea recovered enough to testify against Hazzard at the trial for the death of Claire. Linda Hazzard was convicted of manslaughter and sentenced to hard labor at Washington State Penitentiary. She only served two years and then went to New Zealand with Samuel where she continued to pretend she was a doctor. After the authorities there learned of her past she moved back to Olalla and promptly opened another bogus sanitarium! This new sanitarium burned down though a few years later. Linda Hazzard died in 1938 at the age of 70. The cause of death? Starvation through fasting. You might argue that this was an overdue case of just desserts.

(31) RAYA AND SAKINA (Years Active 1919-1920, Seventeen Victims)

Raya and Sakina were Egyptian serial killers and sisters. They were, along with male husband accomplices, part of a group that killed women in the Labban neighborhood of Alexandria in the early 1900s. Raya and Sakina ran four brothels and many of the victims were usually prostitutes who either worked there or were inquiring about work there. Sometimes the victims were simply female customers who had gone there to sleep with another woman. The victims were restrained, suffocated with a wet cloth, and then had their money and valuables stolen. There were also incidents of victims having their throats slashed.

The jewelry belonging to the victims was usually sold by the sisters and then they shared the profits out among their small gang. The victims were drugged through drinks offered to them so they were not able to offer much resistance. Local articles from the time suggest that over 40 women went missing in the area around the period that Raya and Sakina's deadly activities were taking place. Some of these disappearances probably had nothing to do with Raya and Sakina but a lot of them clearly did. It's difficult therefore to say for sure how many people they actually killed.

It was only when remains and dead bodies began to be found in the area that the net slowly but surely began to tighten around Raya and Sakini. They lived very close to where some remains were found so it was inevitable that they would be investigated sooner or later. The two women and their husbands were put on trial murder in 1921. Sakina in particular was chillingly honest in court. "I myself have cut the throats of six women," she said. "My first victim was called Hanem. I leaned over Hanem as if to whisper in her ear. Soon after death had passed. After a throat-cutting or smothering we took off the jewellery and searched for the valuables, which were divided. I had to look sharp to make sure I was not cheated out of my share."

Ten bodies were found in Sakina's house. The true victim count was clearly a lot higher than this though. The odd thing about these murders is that they clearly hadn't netted Raya and Sakina much in the way of money. The sisters and their husbands lived in abject poverty. All four defendents were convicted and were sentenced to death in 1921. Raya and Sakina became the first Egyptian women to be executed by the modern state of Egypt.

One of the reasons why crime was able to flourish at this time in Egypt was because the British controlled authorities who ran the country were so busy quashing opposition to colonial rule they didn't have much spare time to fight crime. Raya and Sakina were able to evade suspicion for a time because no one suspected that two women could be behind these brutal murders. The thought that women were capable of coldly killing other women was evidently news to the police in Egypt at the time. To this day, tourists in the Labban area often visit the old home of Ray and Sakina. You could say it's sort of like Egypt's version of a Jack the Ripper tour.

(30) BELLE GUNNESS (Years Active 1884–1908, Fourteen Suspected Victims)

Belle Gunness (born 1859) was a Norwegian woman who moved to the United States in the late 19th century. She had a farm in Indiana but any men who went to this farm were seemingly never seen again. Belle Gunness put an ad in the paper looking for a husband but this was one ad you didn't want to respond to. Her life and death is still shrouded in some mystery but there is enough evidence to suggest that Belle Gunness was a very deadly woman and best avoided unless you wanted an early grave.

When she first moved to America she married a Norwegian man and they opened a store. There were four children too. The husband died in a store fire though - which was handy for Belle because she got an insurance payout. She used the money to buy a farm in Indiana and got married again. The new husband didn't last very long though. Mere months later he was dead in what Belle described (with some understatement) as an unfortunate meat grinder accident. Amazingly though, the authorities still didn't seem to suspect any foul play when it came to this mysterious woman.

Belle then placed an ad in the newspaper in an attempt to find another husband. Many men went to the farm after reading the ad but none of them were seen again. You probably had better odds of surviving a tour of duty in Iraq than you did of a trip to the farm of Belle Gunness. In 1908 the farm burned down and the police found the remains of eleven victims - which included Belle's children and a woman's head. Did Belle die in the blaze or did she stage the whole thing to escape? The jury is still out. No one knows what happened. It is often reported that the head found on the farm belonged to Belle Gunness but this was never verified for sure.

Naturally there were unverified sightings of Belle Gunness in the years that followed but her true fate remains a mystery. Ray Lamphere, who worked on Belle's farm, was a suspect in the murders but he was never actually charged (except for arson). It seems plausible (given that many allege he was Belle's lover) that Lamphere might have been an accomplice. Perhaps he decided to kill Belle in the end. Locals who live near the old farm of Belle Gunness often report it to be haunted now. They say you can often hear screams coming the site from where the victims of Belle Gunness perished.

(29) BERTHA GIFFORD (Years Active 1909-1928, Around Seventeen Victims)

Bertha Gifford was born in Morse Mill, Missouri in 1871. She was one of ten children and twice married. Bertha was said to be a beautiful woman in her youth and eventually moved to Catawissa, Franklin County, Missouri. Here she became something of a local legend for her community spirit. Bertha would cook for neighbours and was an excellent chef. If anyone got ill or was feeling under the weather she would selflessly rush to their aid and care for them. In this capacity she even donned a nurses uniform - despite the fact that she wasn't a trained nurse and had no medical qualifications. This didn't stop her though from dispensing medical wisdom and her own solutions to ailments.

There was one other thing about Bertha that the locals seemed to appreciate. She never missed a local funeral. There were few things in life that Bertha loved more than a good funeral. Well, you can probably guess where this story is heading. Naturally, it was none other than Bertha Gifford who was sending all these locals to the graveyard in the first place. In her duties as a 'nurse' and cook she was poisoning all and sundry. It didn't seem to make much difference to Bertha who she killed. She poisoned children and even her own mother in law.

One rather suspicious thing about Bertha, that maybe should have been picked up sooner, was the fact that she sometimes seemed to be visibly irritated and disappointed if one of her 'patients' made a recovery. That, in hindsight, was beyond suspicious. Bertha's tally of victims is impossible to verify for sure but most true crime accounts of her case put the number at seventeen (and this is at the very least). It later transpired that Bertha had a large stash of arsenic at her home because of an alleged rat problem. We obviously know now what she was really using this arsenic for and it had nothing to do with rats.

If someone died under her care (and this obviously happened an awful lot), Bertha would usually say that the victim had died of what she called gastritis. Bertha would always pretend to be some sort of medical expert and, surprisingly, this even seemed to fool genuine doctors for a time. Bertha was finally arrested in 1928 in relation to five suspicious deaths of people she had been caring for. The authorities suspected she had a hand in at least twelve other suspicious deaths in the area but proving this turned out to be very difficult. Bertha's trial only lasted for four days. She was judged to be completely insane and sent to the Missouri State Psychiatric Hospital where she died in 1951 at the age of 79.

(28) MARGARET WATERS (Years Active 1866-1870, Nineteen Suspected Victims)

Margaret Waters was born in London in 1835. Waters was another of those infamous evil Victorian baby farmers (the practice of accepting custody of an infant or child in exchange for payment in late-Victorian Era Britain). Waters starved, neglected, or drugged the babies under her care and is estimated to have killed around nineteen children. Thankfully, the practice of baby farming was outlawed at the start of the 20th century in Britain. It was people like Waters and Amelia Dyer who prompted a change in the law.

Waters took up baby farming after the death of her husband in 1864. She would take in a baby for £10. These babies were illegitimate or simply unwanted. The role of a baby farmer was to care for and look after the babies until they could be found a foster home. However, Margaret Waters deduced that if she simply killed the babies or let them die she could keep all the money herself and wouldn't have any expenditure like food, blankets, and medicine. She would drug the babies with opiates and leave them to starve and perish.

Baby farmer killers like Margaret Waters are among the most disturbing in history because it is unfathomable to normal people how anyone could be so cruel and heartless to innocent children simply for a few extra pennies. After they died, Waters would wrap up the babies and dump them in the street somewhere. The evil activities of Waters soon attracted suspicion and she was arrested after it came to light that she had murdered a sixteen month old boy. The police officer who entered her house described the awful sight that awaited him in the following way - 'Some half-dozen little infants lay together on a sofa, filthy, starving, and stupefied by laudanum.'

After she was arrested, Waters said her crimes were a result of desperation because of the debts she had collected. She was in hock to some nasty money lenders and in desperate need of money. At first, Waters had looked after the babies in the humane and professional manner she was supposed to but - tragically - this didn't last. Waters also had a ruse where she would go out with a baby and ask a child to hold the baby for her while she went in a shop. While the child was holding the baby, Waters would slip away. The babies she abandoned in this way probably ended up in the workhouse in the end but at least they were alive.

Margaret Waters was hanged in 1870 at Horsemonger Lane Gaol in London. She seem calm and composed at the end and said a prayer before her execution. Those who dealt with her in prison found her to be a polite and intelligent woman. That she was had responsible for such awful crimes was unfathomable. It just goes to show you that people will sometimes do the most awful things purely for financial gain. They don't call money the root of all evil for nothing.

(27) DAGMAR OVERBYE (Years Active 1913–1920, 20+ Suspected Victims)

Dagmar Overbye was born in Denmark in 1887. Overbye (who had three children of her own) worked as a child caretaker. This meant that she looked after babies until such time as a family could be found to adopt them. It was basically the old baby farming racket under another name. Overbye opened her own child caretaking business in Copenhagen and seemed to be doing very well. However, she wasn't looking after the babies at all. She was simply killing them to spare herself the expense of looking after them. It is believed that about 180 babies were sent to this child caretaking business. Abortion was illegal in Denmark at the time so there was no shortage of unwanted babies.

Some of the babies were strangled and some were drowned. Overbye would then try and cremate them in her stove. At other times she buried the bodies outside. Overbye's grisly and evil scheme came to an end thanks to a woman named Karoline Aagesen. Aagesen had given her infant daughter to Overbye to look after and find a family but she changed her mind and decided she wanted to get her daughter back. Aagesen went to see Overbye to claim her daughter but Overbye said the child had already been found a family.

Aagesen then asked for the address of the family who had adopted her daughter but Overbye said she couldn't remember where they lived. Aagesen became suspicious of Overbye very quickly and contacted the police. The police went to Overbye's apartment to speak with her and made a grisly discovery. They found the skull and bones of an infant in the stove. When they opened a cupboard they found dozens of charred bone fragments inside. Overbye had no option but to confess to these awful murders. Dagmar Overbye admitted to twenty murders (including one of her own children) but the police could only find sufficient evidence to charge her with nine murders. The real figure is of course unknown.

Most crime historians in Denmark think Dagmar Overbye killed over twenty children. Because she burned and buried remains it was impossible to verify a specific number of deaths. The cremated ashes of her victims were found hidden all over her house. Overbye was sentenced to death but the monarch Christian X overturned this ruling because he didn't believe that women should be executed. As a consequence, Overbye was given life in prison. She died in prison on May the 6th, 1929, at the age of 42. Overbye's awful crimes did at least have one positive note. As a result of this case the Danish government changed the laws on child caretaking so that registered and monitored children's homes took over activities like this from baby farmers.

(26) MIKYUKI ISHIKAWA (Years Active 1944-1948, 100+ Suspected Victims)

When it comes to medical professionals, Miyuki Ishikawa is up there with the worst killers in terms of numbers. Ishikawa (born in 1897) killed more than 103 newborn children in Japan in the late and post-war years. She is known as Oni-Sanba (which translates as Demon Midwife). Ishikawa was a hospital director in the Kotobuki maternity hospital and highly experienced and respected. During the war and in the years that followed a large number of infants ended up in the hospital where Ishikawa was in charge. As you might imagine, Japan was pretty much destroyed in the last years of World War 2 and the death and destruction created many orphans and many destitute transient people who couldn't care for a child.

Many of the parents of these infants had no money (some of them didn't even have homes) and Miyuki Ishikawa found that the hospital was overloaded with babies. However, rather than seek to establish or find places where the overflow of babies could be looked after, Miyuki Ishikawa decided there was nothing she could do for them so she started to allow the babies to die. She simply neglected them on purpose so they would perish. The amount of infants who died as a result of this cold hearted decision is sometimes estimated to be around 160 but the general number of victims is usually credited at around a hundred.

The other staff members at the hospital were outraged when they learned of Ishikawa's conduct and many resigned. There were accomplices though and some doctors participated in forging death certificates. Miyuki Ishikawa even claimed payments from the parents for taking in these infants and allowing them to die. She told the parents she would be saving them money in the long run. In a sense then Miyuki Ishikawa was not completely dissimilar to one of those awful Victorian baby farmer killers. Strange as it might seem the fate of infants at the time was of no great concern to the Japanese authorities. They didn't really seem to care.

Miyuki Ishikawa was finally arrested in 1948 when two police officers found two dead infants and medical tests indicated they had not died of natural causes. This was merely the tip of the iceberg though. There were tends of dozens of dead infants found in the hospital mortuary. The weirdest part of this tale is surely the sentence handed to Miyuki Ishikawa. She was given eight years in prison but then had this sentence halved to four years after an appeal! Miyuki Ishikawa's defence in court was that the parents of these infants were responsible for the deaths by passing them onto the hospital. Incredibly, this defence actually seemed to work and Miyuki Ishikawa attracted some public sympathy.

It remarkable in the case of Miyuki Ishikawa that this cold and heartless woman didn't get a sterner sentence and wasn't more despised in Japan for her awful crimes. She is one of the worst medical killers in history. While her job was not exactly easy it seems clear that she made no real concerted effort to save these babies or find alternative arrangements for them. In the end she was strangely indifferent to their fate and ended up facilitating their deaths by the dozen.

(25) IVANOVA AND OLGA TAMARIN (Years Active - Sometime Up To 1912, 27 Suspected Victims)

Not an awful lot is known about the backgrounds of Ivanova and Olga Tamarin save for the fact they were mother and daughter. Their crimes have only recently surfaced in old newspaper articles of the day but they don't seem to be especially famous in true crime lore. Their crimes apparently took place in Kurdino - which is in Russia. Ivanova and Olga lived in a small house near a forest and well away from the local village. The duo would entice men to their house and then murder them so they could steal money and valuables. Olga, who was seventeen, was the main 'bait' when it came to luring men.

This murderous duo were rather like a mini European version of The Bloody Benders in the way that they killed their victims. They had a special trapdoor and would hit them with blunt objects. Mother and daughter would then dismember and cut the bodies up together. Not only that but they would eat their victims too according to legend. It was the discovery of corpses and bones in the local area that made the police start to take notice of the fact that a number of men seemed to have gone missing in proximity to this village and forest.

A policeman went undercover to investigate and ended up at the Tamarin home - where he soon deduced the smell of death. It is said that Olga tried to kill him but he managed to escape and come back with other officers to arrest them. The two women put up quite a struggle by all accounts before they were finally put in shackles. The police found 27 corpses in the house and money and jewelry belonging to the victims. A number of grisly murder and dissection tools were also discovered.

Ivanova and Olga claimed that they hadn't done this alone and had accomplices in the village. Around 40 men had been recently murdered in the area recently so who knows how many people Ivanova and Olga and their accomplices might really have killed. A large number of people in the village were arrested for alleged participation in these crimes. Ivanova and Olga are said to have been banished to a military prison for their crimes. They occupy a fairly unique position in the history of crime because it's hard to think of too many other serial killing cannibal mother and daughter teams!

(24) MARIA SWANENBURG (Years Active 1880–1883, 23 Verified Victims, Many More Suspected Victims)

Maria Swanenburg was born in Gorinchem, Netherlands, 1839. Known as Goeie Mie (good morning), she is sometimes alleged to have poisoned over one hundred people. Those who have researched her story in Holland believe this figure is exaggerated but there's no doubt that - at the very least - she was a prolific poisoner with dozens of victims. Even a conservative victim estimate would put her near the top table of female serial killers.

Swanenburg killed by slipping arsenic into food and drink. One of her favourite methods was to slip poison into a bowl of porridge. Yes, you can safely say that Maria Swanenburg was the last person in the world you'd want to have some breakfast with. She poisoned both her mother and father and sixteen relatives in all. Swanenburg lived in a destitute sort of area and often worked as a babysitter. Because this area was very poor and people were dying of disease, poverty, and natural causes all the time, her activities didn't really provoke much suspicion for a while.

Swanenburg was never suspected by anyone who knew her because she was considered by everyone to be a kind and generous person. She had a matronly sort of air and was like a beloved aunt in the community. Her motivation for the murders was, in some cases, money. She would poison relatives with life insurance policies and steal the money. She also took the possessions and valuables of others she murdered. Here's the strange thing though. Maria Swanenburg also poisoned people with no life insurance and no money. It was established that even when she stood to make not a single penny from a victim she still poisoned them. She just seemed to be addicted to the act of poisoning someone to death.

The poison was something she'd purchased easily and legally in a store as a way to remove bedbugs. Swanenburg's killing spree came to an end when three members of a family died in suspiciously similar circumstances and a doctor smelled a rat and decided to investigate. The bodies of the family victims were exhumed and examined - verifying that they had been poisoned. Swanenburg was linked to this family and swiftly arrested. Maria Swanenburg confessed to the murders and was taken into permanent custody.

The case recieved tremendous press coverage in the Netherlands. There were lynch mobs out for Maria Swanenburg's blood when the trial began. Her only words during the trial were an appeal for mercy. Swanenburg was sentenced to life in prison and died behind bars in 1915 at the age of 75. It is impossible to tell how many people she tried to poison in her exploits as a serial killer. At least fifty people either became mysteriously ill or died in the area while she was active.

As a result of the Maria Swanenburg case, the law was changed in Holland to make it more difficult to buy dangerous poisons in shops. The policy of taking out life insurance on another person was also changed to make it more difficult and much more scrutinised. The Nederlandsche Panopticum wax museum in Amsterdam later added a figure of Maria Swanenburg to the Chamber of Horrors. She was certainly deadly enough to warrant her place in any waxworks of horror.

(23) LIZZIE HALLIDAY (Years Active 1890s, Five Victims)

Lizzie Halliday was born Eliza Margaret McNally in County Antrim, Ireland. There is some debate as to the year in which she was born but it is usually cited as 1859. When she was a little girl her family moved from Ireland to the United States. Lizzie lived in New York at first and eventually got married a number of times. Her husbands usually died or left her. It is often reported that she tried to poison her fourth husband with arsenic and so had to flee before she could be questioned. Lizzie made her way to Vermont and got married yet again but the marriage didn't last very long. Lizzie vanished only weeks after the marriage.

She had by now made her way to Philadelphia - where it is believed Lizzie had some Irish friends who were able to offer her a bed for a few nights and some financial assistance. Lizzie decided to open up a shop in the city and then set fire to it for the insurance money. This scam evidently did not fool the authorities and Lizzie was sentenced to two years in prison for fraud. After her release, Lizzie was employed as a housekeeper in New York by Paul Halliday, a seventy-year-old farmer and widower. Despite the fact that she was decades older than Halliday, Lizzie married him.

The decision to marry Lizzie turned out to be a disaster for Paul Halliday. First she burned down his barn - killing her husband's son John in the process. This wasn't even the first time she had set fire to the barn. Lizzie had done this before. The death of John was clearly no accident as Lizzie is said to have disliked him. After a spell in an asylum, she returned to Paul Halliday and killed him. Lizzie is said to have mutilated his body afterwards. After Paul Halliday went missing a number of neighbours became suspicious of Lizzie and contacted the police. A search of the farm was undertaken and the bodies of two women were found in the barn. They had both been shot. The women were Margaret and Sarah McQuillan. Both of these women were people Lizzie knew from New York.

Soon after, the butchered body of Paul Halliday was found in the floorboards of the house. Lizzie had been racking up an escalating body count before her grisly deeds were discovered. This case was a sensation in the newspapers at the time and many wondered if Lizzie had bumped off some of her (many) previous husbands too. For this reason the victim count of Lizzie Halliday is sometimes put at six rather than four. The true figure is impossible to verify though. Five seems a reasonable guess.

Because of the ruthless barbarity of her crimes there was even speculation that Lizzie might be Jack the Ripper. "Do they think I am an Elephant?" said Lizzie when asked if she was Jack the Ripper. "That was done by a man." Lizzie was convicted of murder and sentenced to death in the electric chair. However this death sentence was commuted sentence to life in a mental institution after a medical commission declared her insane. In 1906, she killed a nurse at a hospital for criminally insane by stabbing the nurse with pair of scissors. Lizzie Halliday died in 1918. She was one of the craziest and most dangerous female serial killers in history.

(22) KATERINA Z KOMAROVA (Years Active

1540s-1550s, Twenty+ Suspected Victims)

Kateřina z Komárova, whose birth date is uncertain, was a Czech noblewoman who became an infamous figure for the mistreatment on servants and serfs on her estate. She was convicted for fourteen murders but might have killed as many as thirty people. Komárova was married to Jan Bechyně - who was quite a big cheese when it came to power and politics. He was essentially a count and had judicial, political, and military power over a large region.

Because of his duties, Jan Bechyně spent a lot of time away from the family estate and this was bad news for the servants because they were left at the mercy of Kateřina z Komárova. She was said to have tortured her servants by means of cruel punishments that left many of them dead. If you only committed a minor transgression on the estate you were still given a horrendously harsh punishment. Komárova would cut people with knives and put salt in the wounds. It is said that she poured boiling hot butter over some servants as a punishment. Servants had both boiling hot water and ice cold water thrown over them as punishment.

Stories of Komárova's brutal treatment of the servants eventually began to abound in the region and a local Dean got involved in the case. However, Komárova's husband threatened to sue the Dean for even daring to suggest that his wife had been responsible for such awful things. Eventually a trial of sorts was arranged for the servants to tell their side of the story but they were so terrified of Komárova they refused at first to speak of her crimes.

It took one brave serf to speak up though and pretty soon they were all coming forward with tales about the cruelty of Komárova. She eventually confessed to killing fourteen serfs but the true figure was almost certainly higher than that. Komárova didn't seem to express any remorse for her crimes or ever give the impression that she felt she had done anything wrong. As a punishment she was thrown into the Mihulka tower at Prague Castle to starve to death. This happened in around two weeks.

(21) MARIAM SOULAKIOTIS (Years Active 1939-1951, 25+ Suspected Victims)

Mariam Soulakiotis was born in Keratea, Greece in 1883. Soulakiotis was a former factory worker who took control of the Peukovounogiatrissas Monastery and became known as Mother Rasputin for her crimes. The monastery was something of an offshoot and of the Old Calendarist Eastern Orthodox Christian variety. Soulakiotis simply manipulated religion as a means to make money. She would persuade wealthy women to join the convent and then embezzle their money and estates. Torture was rife in the convent and over two dozen people perished.

'Aside from swindling her disciples,' wrote Michael Newton, 'Mariam [Soulakiotis] dominated every aspect of their lives, cutting off their contact with relatives, caging some like animals, resorting to starvation, flogging, and torture to purge new recruits of their "demons." No doctors were permitted on the grounds, and many recruits who entered the commune were never seen again. A mother from Thebes joined the cult with her four daughters; all five were dead within six months of their arrival on the Mount of Pines. Nocturnal passers-by reported screams and moaning from the compound. One night, two drunken villagers scaled the fence and found an elderly woman chained to a wall, but she declined their help and the intruders kept their observation to themselves.'

Soulakiotis was said to have appropriated dozens of properties from victims of the convents and amassed a large collection of jewelry and valuables from those who she fleeced. No one really knows how many people might have been killed in this horror convent. Her refusal to admit doctors to the convent is widely believed to have contributed to the deaths of tens of dozens of children who she tried to treat in the convent herself (despite having no medical knowledge or training) or simply neglected. Mariam Soulakiotis was an absolute monster. She took advantage of religious beliefs and harmed or injured countless people simply as a way to make money.

It took the authorities a while to catch up with Mariam Soulakiotis. "The women are socially dangerous crackpots and have been very clever in giving us the runaround," said the Greek Justice Ministry at the time. "But one day they'll make a slip, as all criminals usually do, and we will catch them. Those crazy females claim that will someday go to heaven, but if we meet up with them, we'll show them what hell is like first." Soulakiotis was finally put on trial in 1953 and sentenced to ten years in prison. Four years was added to her sentence this same year for various other charges. Soulakiotis died in Averoff Prison in 1954. She was 61 years-old. She has been called the wickedest woman of the 20th century.

(20) MARY ANN COTTON (Years Active 1857-1872, 20+ Suspected Victims)

Mary Ann Cotton was born in Sunderland in 1832. She tends to be known as The Black Widow in true crime lore. Cotton has sometimes been called Britain's first serial killer. It's safe to say that if you were ever offered a cup of tea by Mary Ann Cotton you'd be advised to decline unless you enjoy a large dose of arsenic in your PG Tips. Her childhood was fairly uneventful save for her father dying in a mining accident. She spent some time in a boarding school and was said to be a sensible girl who always took a great pride in her appearance. This last quality was evident in her choice of profession. Mary trained to become a dressmaker.

In 1852, Mary married a man named William Mowbray. They had several children but few of them survived. Not all of these births were registered so it was difficult to keep track of exactly how many children they had and how many died. In those days the sad premature death of babies and infants was not uncommon so these deaths were not considered suspicious. Mary's husband William died in 1865 because of a stomach ailent. William was insured and Mary received a nice little payment upon his death as a result. Mary's second husband was George Ward. He also died though - once again allowing Mary to collect an insurance payment. The cause of death was cited as cholera but the suddenness of his departure from this vale of tears was rather surprising.

Husband number three for Mary was a widower named James Robinson. Meanwhile, Mary's mother died suddenly after complaining of stomach pains. Yes, you might say that all these sudden deaths in relation to Mary were becoming rather too suspicious. Mary's daughter and two of Robinson's children (from his previous marriage) then all suddenly died in quick succession. James Robinson had noticed at this juncture how Mary kept trying to persuade him to take out life insurance. He decided to boot her out of the house after discovering that she had been pawning his valuables and running up debts.

In 1870, Mary nabbed husband number four when she married Frederick Cotton (from whom she obviously got her last name). Mary was pretty destitute by this point after the collapse of her last marriage and so was desperate to find a new husband. This new marriage was actually illegal because she wasn't even officially divorced from her last husband. Mary wasn't the greatest wife in the world it has to be said. She found out that an old flame named Joseph Nattrass lived nearby and so went off to woo him. As for Frederick Cotton, you can probably guess what happened to him. That's right. He died of a stomach complaint.

Frederick Jr, the child of her last husband, then suddenly died as did Joseph Nattrass - who was Mary's lodger at the time. In 1872, one of Mary Cotton's surviving stepchildren Charles Cotton died suddenly and mysteriously. Mary had told a parish official that Charles 'was in the way' of her future plans. When the apparently healthy Charles dropped dead, the local parish official became highly suspicious (not before time you might argue!) of Mary.

Mary tried to collect the life insurance on Charles but the authorities would not release the money until a medical investigation had taken place. When the body of Charles Cotton was exhumed, arsenic was found in his system. At the trial which followed, Mary was sentenced to death but insisted she was innocent. 'After conviction,' wrote The Times, 'the wretched woman exhibited strong emotion but this gave place in a few hours to her habitual cold, reserved demeanour and while she harbours a strong conviction that the royal clemency will be extended towards her, she staunchly asserts her innocence of the crime that she has been convicted of.'

Mary Ann Cotton was hanged at Durham County Gaol in March 1873. The hanging was rather botched and she ended up slowly choking to death on the rope. Of Mary Ann Cotton's thirteen estimated children, only two survived her. She had killed the vast majority of her family. The notorious crimes of Mary Ann Cotton inspired a nursery rhyme of the era.

Mary Ann Cotton, she's dead and she's rotten
Lying in bed with her eyes wide open.
Sing, sing, oh what should I sing?
Mary Ann Cotton, she's tied up with string.
Where, where? Up in the air.
Selling black puddings, a penny a pair.

Mary Ann Cotton, she's dead and forgotten,
Lying in bed with her bones all rotten.
Sing, sing, what can I sing?
Mary Ann Cotton, tied up with string.

(19) GEORGIA TANN (Years Active 1924–1950, 50+ Victims)

Georgia Tann was born in 1891 in Philadelphia, Mississippi. As a young woman she was social worker and then worked at the Mississippi Children's Home Society. Tann was apparently fired from this establishment and along with her (secret) lover Ann Atwood landed on her feet when she became Executive Secretary at the Tennessee Children's Home Society. In those days it was a lot easier to adopt children than it is today. Adoption was fairly inexpensive and background checks were minimal. This naturally seems rather chilling to us today and, unfortunately, it often was.

Tann, along with various accomplices who included corrupt judges and criminal nurses, would basically abduct children to put up for adoption. Many of these children suffered dreadful abuse (not least from Tann herself - who was a child molester). To the outside world though Tann was a nice old lady who was considered to be an expert on child care. First Lady Eleanor Roosevelt even praised Tann. The actual truth was rather different.

Georgia Tann was involved in trafficking thousands of babies - many of them were stolen. Some of these babies ended up with celebrity clients like Joan Crawford (watch the film Mommie Dearest to get an alleged taste of how this particular adoption turned out). While the babies and children were awaiting adoption they were left at the Tennessee Children's Home Society. Many of the children there were neglected, sexually molested, or allowed to die. We don't really know how many deaths Georgia Tann's business was responsible for but some have suggested it might be in the hundreds.

'Many were drugged and starved by Tann and her employees,' wrote Criminal Element. 'Medical treatment was withheld. Several, perhaps hundreds, died from neglect and were buried in unmarked graves without death certificates. It has been reported that Memphis had the highest child mortality rate in the country at one time, much of which was attributed to Tann's neglect. Even those who were desirable weren't safe. Many reported later that they had been repeatedly assaulted by Tann and her employees, often strung up by the wrists while punished or sexually molested.'

Although some of the babies and children were found decent homes there were also cases of girls being adopted by pedophiles or boys being adopted to use as slave labour. How did this awful state of affairs manage to exist? The simple fact is that Georgia Tann was friends with the local Judge and the Mayor. She had influence. As a consequence of this, no one scrutinised her affairs too closely. There was little paperwork in the adoptions so the real source of these children was masked. Tann is believed to have made over one million dollars from stealing and selling babies.

In 1950, Tennessee governor Gordon Browning launched an investigation into Georgia Tann after hearing stories about her adoption business. However, Tann died of cancer at the age of 59 only days before charges were due to be brought against her. Because of this there was no trial or prosecution and much of Tann's life is still shrouded in a degree of mystery. There were no prosecutions and - sadly - none of the black market children were returned to their real mothers. The dead children and babies found in the Children's Home in unmarked graves could not be identified. In 2015, a memorial to Tann's hundreds of victims was placed in Memphis's Elmwood Cemetery. Georgia Tann was a truly awful woman and she had been hiding in plain sight all along.

(18) PIROSKA JANCSO LADANYI (Years Active 1953-1954, Five Victims)

Piroska Jancsó Ladányi was born in the Hungarian town of Törökszentmiklós in 1934. It is sometimes said that you don't get necrophile female serial killers like Dennis Nilsen or Gary Ridgway but this isn't true at all. Piroska Jancsó Ladányi is a case in point. She had a rough childhood and was abused by Red Army soldiers (Hungary was at this time an occupied puppet state of the Soviet Union). Piroska was said to be cruel to animals from a young age and is also alleged to have engaged in incest with her brother. It was a messed up start in life to say the least.

Piroska didn't have much schooling but she enjoyed reading novels and was said to be of above average intelligence. Like many serial killers she also had early convictions for theft. Her first victim was eleven year-old Marika Komáromi in 1953. Piroska isolated the child and then strangled her with chicken wire at a farmhouse. She then undressed the body and sexually abused the corpse. After she was satisfied, Piroska dragged the body outside with rope and hid it underneath some metal sheets. The other victims were killed in 1954. The next victim was a thirteen year-old girl named Hoppál. Piroska strangled the girl and then sexually abused the body. Piroska said she inserted a carrot into herself while she was doing this. Hoppál was then thrown into a well.

Irene Simon, who was seventeen, was the next victim. Piroska killed this girl because she was having a sexual relationship with her and didn't want anyone to find out. She decided the best solution to that worry would be to simply murder her lover. Irene Simon was strangled and thrown down a well. The next victim was thirteen year-old Marika Botos - who was on holiday with her grandmother. Once again, Piroska isolated the girl, lured her away, and strangled her before sexually abusing the corpse. Katalin Szőke, also thirteen, was the next victim. She was strangled with a belt strap before Piroska used the corpse to satiate her warped necrophile sexual desires.

Piroska took the clothes and belongings of the victims and sold them. By this time the deaths were starting to attract attention and a number of theories were juggled by the police. Soviet soldiers and gypsies were the main suspects. The exploits of Piroska were ended by a 21 year-old woman named István Balázsi. Piroska tried to strangle Balázsi but she escaped and fled to the police. The police investigation eventually led them to the well where Piroska had dumped her victims.

At first, Piroska tried to pretend that male accomplices had done the murders but this was a blatant lie. She even implicated a Soviet soldier. This made the investigation difficult for the police because they obviously didn't have much authority over the Red Army. Piroska eventually came clean though and offered a full confession. She admitted that the murders were sexually motivated and said she had always been attracted to girls.

Piroska claimed that her mother was aware of the murders (it is said that it was Piroska's mother who had the idea of selling the clothes of the victims for money) and so at the initial trial her mother got two years in prison while Piroska was sentenced to death. After public outcry, Piroska's mother got a new sentence where she was sentenced to death too! This was commuted to life in prison though. There was no such luck for Piroska. In 1954 she was killed by hanging in the courtyard of the Szolnok prison. The gates of the prison were opened that day so that members of the public could come in and watch the execution.

(17) HELENE JEGADO (Years Active 1883-1851, 30+ Suspected Victims)

Hélène Jégado was born near Lorient in Brittany in 1803. She came from a family of servants and after the death of her mother was sent to assist two aunts in various places. Jégado worked as a servant or cook in various houses and even religious retreats. She did though have one compulsive weakness which she couldn't seem to resist at times. Hélène Jégado was a poisoner who is believed to possibly killed as many as 36 people in all. Jégado poisoned for the first time in 1833 when she was employed by a priest. Several members of the household were poisoned - including the aforementioned priest. Even the visiting sister of Hélène Jégado was poisoned.

Hélène Jégado did not attract any suspicion at this time because her grief at the deaths and poisonings was so convincing. She was clearly a highly accomplished actress.

Jégado stayed at various places in the months and weeks that followed and death and illness was (suspiciously) never too far away. She poisoned her aunt, her landlady and the landlady's daughter, and later a widow she rented a room from. In 1935 she was employed at a new house and our deaths soon abounded.

It is said that Hélène Jégado even joined a convent. As you might imagine, as soon she started at the convent the nuns started dropping like flies. Oddly, Hélène Jégado apparently did not poison anyone from 1841 to 1849. It is unusual for serial killers to have long 'rest periods' like this but not unheard of. In 1850, Hélène Jégado began working for Théophile Bidard, who was a professor at the University of Rennes. When the servants started to fall ill and in some cases perished, suspicion finally began to fall on Hélène Jégado because she was usually the one caring for them at the time of their death.

Like many notorious poisoners, Hélène Jégado would offer to care for victims so she could maintain control over them and finish them off. When the local authorities decided to speak to Hélène Jégado they found it suspicious that she immediately announced her innocence before they'd even accused her of anything or explained why they had come to speak to her. Hélène Jégado was a difficult person to convict because they found no arsenic in her possessions and she had no clothing, valuables, or jewelry from her victims. She was either good at hiding her tracks or simply wasn't a financial serial killer.

It is often suggested that Hélène Jégado killed people who irritated her. This is certainly not uncommon in these strange and baffling cases of serial poisoners. They often seem to poison and kill people for fairly petty things like slights or little arguments. Hélène Jégado, though suspected of dozens of murders, was put on trial on three counts of murder and found guilty. Jégado gave an eccentric performance in court. She ranted and raved and insisted that she'd never poisoned anyone in her life. Her protestations of innocence did not stand up to too much scrutiny in court. She was executed by guillotine in front of a large crowd of onlookers on the Champ-de-Mars in Rennes in 1852.

(16) THE FINCHLEY BABY FARMERS (Years Active 1900-1902, Dozens of Suspected Murders)

Amelia Sach (born 1873) and Annie Walters (born 1869) were two women who became known as The Finchley Baby Farmers. These two women conspired to murder babies in order to make money from the Victorian practice of baby farming. Amelia Sach started a business where babies who needed adoption could be left with her for a fee. Annie Walters would then poison the babies and dispose of them. Sach was married and a fairly respected woman (at least to the unsuspecting world at large) while much less is known about the background of Walters. Walters was deemed to be of very low intelligence and was the one who did the 'dirty work' in this evil scheme.

Many of the babies that these two women dealt with were said to be the illegitimate children of servant girls and maids. There was a great stigma to having a child out of wedlock in the Victorian era and this created a need for women to look after unwanted infants until a home could be found for them. This allowed evil women like Amelia Dyer and the Finchley Baby Farmers to take advantage. They would collect the fee for taking in a baby and then kill the baby so that they didn't incur any further expense looking after them.

It should be noted though that the vast majority of baby farmers were kind and decent women who looked after the babies as if they were their own children. The likes of Sach and Walters were tragic aberrations. What made it quite difficult to weed out murderous baby farmers was the fact that in this era a lot of infants and children died of disease or illness anyway. If an infant died, although tragic, it wasn't something that was especially uncommon.

It was the stupidity of Annie Walters that brought this evil duo to the attention of the authorities. Walters took a baby girl (which was actually a boy but Walters didn't seem to have noticed) home with her and showed the child off to the neighbours. However, the neighbours couldn't fail to notice that the infant disappeared soon after. Walters did the same thing again with a little girl and the authorities decided to investigate. It was rather odd and chilling that Walters seemed to be affectionate towards these infants in the company of her neighbours but then killed them as part of the baby farming scheme. Talk about Jekyll & Hyde.

The two women were (despite their predictable claims of innocence) sentenced to death for murdering the babies in their charge. The hangman who executed the two women later wrote - 'These two women were baby farmers of the worst kind and were both repulsive in type. They had literally to be carried to the scaffold and protested to the end against their sentences.' The bodies of Amelia Sach and Annie Walters were buried in Holloway Prison after their execution. When the prison was rebuilt in 1971, the bodies had to be exhumed and moved elsewhere.

(15) JANE TOPPAN (Years Active 1895–1901, 31+ Suspected Victims)

Jane Toppan was born in Boston in 1854. She was known as The Angel of Death. Toppan murdered at least 31 people with lethal injections in her duties as a nurse. Her parents were Irish immigrants and life was not exactly plain sailing for Jane Toppan as a child. Her mother died of tuberculosis and Jane Toppan's father was said to be so crazy that he once tried to sew up one of his eyelids. Jane Toppan was a bright girl though and entered medical school in 1885.

She was known as Jolly Jane to her colleagues because she was always laughing and smiling. Everyone seemed to like her. She worked at Cambridge Hospital in Massachusetts and developed a fondness for working with patients who were sick or elderly. Jane Toppan first attracted mild suspicion in her medical duties because she was completely obsessed with autopsies. She was absolutely fascinated with death and loved going to the morgue. Jane Toppan used her patients at the hospital to experiment with the drugs morphine and atropine. She would vary the doses to see what reaction occurred in the patient. Naturally, she created bogus medical charts for her patients to disguise what she was actually doing.

Jane Toppan is said to have got a sexual thrill from her murders. She said she even climbed into bed with one patient she had just killed. In 1889, she worked at the Massachusetts General Hospital and continued to murder patients with overdoses. However, her murders were not just confined to the medical world. In 1895 she killed her landlord by poisoning and also murdered his wife. Jane Toppan then killed her sister Elizabeth with strychnine. You didn't have to be in hospital to be at risk from Jane Toppan. She would murder people anywhere given half a chance.

In 1901, Jane Toppan was hired as a private nurse to look after an elderly man named Alden Davis. You can probably guess what happened next. Yes, she murdered this man. But she didn't stop there. She also murdered his sister and two daughters. The relatives of the victims were understandably suspicious of Jane Toppan after these tragic and sudden deaths. They arranged for a medical test on the youngest daughter and the tests concluded the reason for death was poison. After she was taken into custody, Jane Toppan confessed to many murders.

Toppan told the police that she was perfectly sane and always knew exactly what she was doing. She said to the police - "That is my ambition, to have killed more people — more helpless people — than any man or woman who has ever lived." Toppan told the police that she experienced a thrill from having absolute power over patients and enjoyed taking them to the brink of death and then reviving them - and so on. Despite her claim that she was perfectly sane, it was clearly obvious that Jane Toppan was not sane in the least. Jane Toppan was so disturbed she had even poisoned herself once to appear ill and attract sympathy from a prospective boyfriend.

We will never know exactly how many people she actually killed. By any standards, Jane Toppan was completely ruthless. She once poisoned her best friend so that she could have her friend's job as a matron. Jane Toppan would kill literally anyone given the chance. As for explanations for why this woman became a compulsive killer, Jane Toppan was once jilted at the alter when she was supposed to get married. This is speculated to have been one of the sources of her anger and mental instability. "If I had been a married woman, I probably would not have killed all of those people," she said. "I would have had my husband, my children and my home to take up my mind."

Jane Toppan was found not guilty of her crimes by reasons of insanity and committed for life in the Taunton Insane Hospital. She died in 1938 at the age of 84. There was a rather dark irony when Jane Toppan was sent to the Taunton Insane Hospital. At one point, she refused to eat anything at the hospital and complained that someone was trying to poison her!

(14) CATALINA DE LOS RIOS Y LISPERGUER (Years Active 1622-1660, 40+ Alleged Victims)

Catalina de los Ríos y Lisperguer was born in 1604 in Santiago. She was known as La Quintrala because of her flaming red hair. Catalina is a mythic figure in Chile and held up as an object lesson in how power can corrupt. She was an aristocrat and famously cruel to those who served under her. Catalina was suspected of the death of her father Gonzalo de los Ríos in 1622 by feeding him a poisoned dish of chicken. Though she got married and had a son (who died at a young age) she had many lovers and is said to have stabbed one of these to death in her bed. A man named Enrique Enríquez de Guzmán also related a tale in which he claimed that Catalina had attempted to murder him.

When her husband died, Catalina was left in charge of a number of plantations and many slaves. She is said to have tortured and killed a number of slaves but because she had the money to bribe local officials she was able to avoid any investigation. At one point a number of slaves revolted due to their harsh treatment and attempted to flee into the hills. Catalina had to arrange a manhunt to capture them again. Naturally, these slaves received harsh punishments for having the temerity to make a run for it.

When a cleric raised objections to the way Catalina treated her slaves she is said to have tried to kill him to ensure his silence. The awful conditions on the plantations could not be kept a secret forever though and eventually the Bishop Salcedo ordered that an investigation must take place. Officials were sent to examine the conditions on the plantations and when it was established that mistreatment and cruelty abounded, Catalina was taken to Santiago and put on trial for forty murders.

The verdict? Well, there wasn't one. Catalina literally bribed her way out of trouble with money and was eventually released without any charges. Years later there was another attempt to put her on trial but she'd already died by this point. She had died in 1665. Catalina gave away huge sums of money before she died - which suggests she was worried about getting sent 'down below' for her crimes after death. It was said that after her houses were later auctioned off no one wanted to live in them because they were superstitious and about the dark aura such a notorious figure might leave behind.

'La Quintrala,' wrote AncientOrigins, 'even though she was born only a few years before the death of Countess Bathory , and half a world away, still shared a lot of traits with her. Their cruelty, the inherent urge to kill and torment, and the magnanimity of their rule over those of lesser status, all show us glimpses into the minds of people born with the desire to kill. Her crimes never fully brought to light, and her victims never properly named, but Catalina de los Ríos y Lisperguer will go down in history as one of the cruelest female murderers, and one of the earliest serial killers. Her cold-blooded and often unwarranted murders hint at a pathological urge, which provides much insight into the workings of a killer's mind. But the signs of remorse and fear she showed before her death, with a sudden adherence to the church and the Order of St. Augustine and large sums donated to the church, do not wash away the awfulness of her crimes. And it is these very crimes that place La Quintrala shoulder to shoulder with some of the world's deadliest women.'

(13) LILA GLADYS YOUNG (Years Active 1928-1947, 100+ Victms)

Lila Gladys Young was born Lila Coolen at Fox Point, Nova Scotia, in 1899. When she was in her twenties she married a man named William Peach Young. William Peach Young is said to have worked as a chiropractor in Chicago in the early years of their marriage and the couple had five children in all. In the late 1920s, the couple set up the Ideal Maternity Home (previously named Life and Health Sanitarium) in East Chester, Nova Scotia. The home offered maternity care and placements of children from unmarried mothers. The Ideal Maternity Home was basically a lingering continuation of the awful Victorian baby farming business.

Lila Gladys Young was a midwife at the home and said to be famously rough in her treatment of the mothers and babies. She was a stern and unemotional sort of woman. Lila Gladys Young cut all sorts of corners in her desire to turn a profit. If a mother didn't have enough cash to pay their fees they were put to work as glorified slave labour. The Youngs also saved on medical bills by not employing any real doctors. Lila Gladys Young would naturally deliver all the babies herself.

The infant mortality rate at the Ideal Maternity Home was way above the national average in Canada. Any baby unlikely to be found a home was usually starved to death. The Youngs used pine butter boxes as makeshift coffins to save money. Victims of the home are therefore called Butterbox Babies in retrospectives of this case. A handyman who worked at the home later said that over a hundred babies were buried in a field owned by Lila's parents. The babies were left in a tool shed until they could be buried.

In 1934 the Nova Scotia Department of Public Welfare began an investigation into Lila Gladys Young and her husband but this proved complex to say the least. The Youngs were said to be very influential and had a lot of friends in politics and local government. The Youngs were charged with manslaughter in 1936 but then managed to clear themselves on these charges. In 1946 Public Health Officials investigated the Ideal Maternity Home and found awful conditions. The place was filthy and the babies were grossly undernourished and sleeping in dirty bedding. The home was consequently shut down by the authorities.

However, the Youngs were not going down without a fight. They continued to operate without a licence while they appealed the case. When they were then found guilty of violation of the Maternity Boarding House Act and operating without a licence they only received a modest fine. In 1946 they were convicted of illegally selling babies to four American couples and William Peach Young was convicted of perjury. The final nail in the coffin of the Youngs came when Lila tried to sue a newspaper and all manner of evidence against her was thrown in the public realm. The Youngs, now bankrupt, fled to Quebec.

William Young died of cancer just before Christmas, 1962. Lila Young died of leukemia in 1967 at the age of 70. They were awful people who never received the punishment they deserved. Who knows how many innocent babies died as a result of their dreadful business. Some estimates put at the figure at between 400 and 600. Survivors of the Ideal Maternity Home continued to meet as adults many years after the case to support one another.

(12) THE ANGEL MAKERS OF NAGYREV (Years Active 1914-1929, Fifty+ Victims)

The Angel Makers of Nagyrév were a group of woman in Hungry who poisoned to death a large collection of husbands in the village of Nagyrév. How many they killed is not known for sure. Some estimates claim they poisoned 300 men. Even the most conservative estimates though would put the number of victims at around forty or fifty. The ringleader of this group was a midwife named Júlia Fazekas. At the time, the tradition in this village was that the parents of women chose the husband for their daughter. This meant that teenage brides were married off to men that they hadn't chosen themselves and in many cases didn't like very much.

This custom obviously entrapped a lot of women in unhappy marriages. Sometimes they were married off to men who turned out to be abusive or drunks. This was mitigated somewhat by the First World War. Women in unhappy marriages quite enjoyed the fact that their husbands were away fighting and in many cases enjoyed affairs. These affairs were much more to their liking because, unlike their marriages, they had actually been allowed to choose their lovers themselves. However, after the war the husbands all came home and a number of women found themselves back in the unhappy marriage they hadn't even wanted in the first place.

It was Júlia Fazekas who came up with a solution to the problem of unhappy wives in arranged marriages. She suggested they simply murder their husbands by boiling flypaper and skimming off the arsenic residue. The women in the village soon got the hang of the poisoning lark the persuasive Fazekas had proposed and local husbands began dropping like (ahem) flies. There was only one problem though. They didn't stop at husbands. Soon they were poisoning parents, lovers, and even sons. Generally anyone that annoyed them got a dose of arsenic.

Nagyrév became known as 'murder district' because there were so many sudden deaths in the area. Now, you might wonder why none of this was raised any suspicion and why no action was taken by the authorities for so many years. There were a number of reasons for this. The first is that the village didn't actually have a doctor. Júlia Fazekas, as a midwife, was actually considered to be the main medical expert in the village and she obviously wasn't going to say or do anything that would threaten the dark secret of this town as she was the mastermind behind it.

The second reason is that the cousin of Júlia Fazekas was the village clerk in charge of handling the death certificates. Fazekas obviously, with her influence over the clerk, made sure that these deaths were put down to natural causes. The poisonings went on for over a decade until they were put to a stop. There are a number of conflicting explanations for why the women of Nagyrév were finally rumbled. Some say that a doctor visited the village and found arsenic in the body of a dead man. Other reports say that some of the wives in the village were caught in the act of poisoning husbands.

Another claim is that one of the villagers exposed the dark secret of the village by writing an anonymous letter to a newspaper. However it happened though, the murders in the village were eventually uncovered and a number of exhumations took place. Twelve women in the village received prison sentences and two were executed. Thirty eight women in all were arrested. As for Júlia Fazekas, she didn't stick around to explain herself or take the blame. She hung herself in 1929.

(11) DARYA NIKOLAYEVNA SALTYKOVA (Years Active 1757-1764, 100+ Suspected Victims)

Darya Nikolayevna Saltykova was born in the Russian Empire in 1730. Saltykova was a Russian noble and prolific serf killer who tortured and murdered people by the dozen on her estate. She had married Gleb Alexeyevich Saltykov and his death left her a wealthy woman with a large estate. At 26 she was one of the richest widows in the country and had 600 serfs on her estate. It is said that when she was spurned by a lover she went haywire and started taking out her frustration on her serfs.

Saltykova only killed a couple of male serfs. The overwhelming majority of her victims were female. She seemed to have it in for young girls in particular. The serfs had their bones broken and boiling water poured over them. Some were stripped naked and thrown out into subzero temperatures to freeze to death. They were whipped and had objects thrown at them. Saltykova was simply a sadist who seemed to derive satisfaction from being cruel to the serfs. The fact that she was killing them by the dozen didn't bother her in the least.

When complaints about the estate began to abound there was no action against Saltykova at first because she was very wealthy and influential. However, the relatives of the victims were very brave and persistent in drawing attention to the awful crimes going on at the estate and a petition was brought before Empress Catherine II. Saltykova was arrested in 1762 and the Collegium of Justice began an investigation.

This investigation estimated that 138 people had suspiciously died on the estate. Saltykova was found guilty of causing these deaths but she couldn't be executed because the death penalty had been abolished at the time. Darya Nikolayevna Saltykova was chained to a platform in Moscow with a sign around her neck which said she was a murderer and torturer. The public were allowed to come and 'view' her. After this humiliation she was thrown in prison where she died in 1801.

(10) FELIICITAS SANCHEZ AGUILLON (Years Active 1924–1950, 45+ Victims)

Felícitas Sánchez Aguillón was born in Cerro Azul, Veracruz, Mexico in 1890. Her terrible infamy lent her a number of titles - the most common of which are The Female Ripper of Colonia Roma and The Human Crusher of Little Angels. As a young woman she became a nurse although she was not the most maternal of people. She got married and had twin daughters but she was so indifferent to her children she arranged to have them adopted.

Aguillón eventually moved to Mexico City where she began performing illegal abortions and got involved in the baby farming trade. Any babies that she couldn't get any money for she simply killed. She would drug or strangle the unwanted babies and then dump them in a river or sewer. The babies in her care were treated abominably. She made them sleep on the floor and fed them food that had gone off. They were given cold baths.

The awful crimes of Aguillón were uncovered in 1941 when the building in the Roma neighbourhood where she was based began to experience problems with its drains. Plumbers were sent to rectify the problem and they found things that were grisly and disturbing beyond words. In the pipe they found rotted meat and greased and bloodied rags. They also found a human skull that belonged to a baby. Aguillón is believed to have murdered between forty and fifty babies.

She was able to keep her wicked scheme secret for as long as she did because one of her accomplices was a plumber. In the end though the drains simply became too clogged. Neighbours are said to have become suspicious of Aguillón because a thick pungent black smoke would sometimes come from her rooms.

This was clearly a result of her burning the bodies of her victims. Aguillón would sometimes chop the babies up after she had killed them and hide them on garbage dumps.

When the police searched the rooms of Felícitas Sánchez Aguillón they found a number of religious artifacts and photographs of children. She had fled with a lover but thankfully was captured a day later. Felícitas Sánchez Aguillón was found to be a delusional woman who seemed to think she was on some sort of religious mission. She was clearly not the full shilling. Aguillón retreated into a childlike state in custody as the investigation developed.

It was said that Aguillón had some baby adoption clients who were famous and involved in politics. The authorities were eager to get these names but Aguillón committed suicide by an overdose before the full details of her baby farming business were gathered. She was 50 years old. Aguillón had another daughter and husband by the time of her death. Her husband was convicted of being an accomplice and her daughter was placed in foster care. By any standards, Felícitas Sánchez Aguillón was one of the most heartless killers imaginable.

(9) IRINA GAIDAMACHUK (Years Active 2002-2010, Seventeen Victims)

Irina Gaidamachuk was born in 1972 in the town of Nyagan, Khanty–Mansi Autonomous Okrug, in the Soviet Union. Gaidamachuk was said to have developed an alcohol problem at an absurdly young age. She married a man named Yuri as a young woman and had two children. Irina Gaidamachuk was considered by the world at large to be a normal and decent women. She was popular in her community and used to help out at her daughter's school. However, her addiction to alcohol seemed to tilt her into a brutal rampage of murder. She would later say that her husband Yuri would never give her any money to buy vodka. Irina decided she would take matters into her own hands in the most savage fashion.

In the Urals region, she began posing as a social worker in order to gain access to the homes of frail and elderly victims. Once inside she would batter them to death with an axe or hammer and then steal what money they had. The money she stole from these murders was what you might describe as slim pickings. Irina Gaidamachuk murdered seventeen people but only gathered a total of about $1,000 from these victims combined. After she killed someone she would write a number on the wall to count how many she had killed. There were cases of Gaidamachuk trying to set fire to the homes of the people she had just killed but neighbours were able to put out the fires before they got out of control.

The police investigation into the murders was rather incompetent to say the least. The police only considered male suspects at first because they refused to believe that a woman was capable of such brutal murders. They then, ludicrously, developed a theory (upon hearing eyewitness accounts of a possible suspect) that the killer might be a man dressed as a woman! A similar thing (as we shall see) happened with the serial killer Juana Barraza. In both cases it seemed to take the police a long time to deduce that a woman might be responsible for the murders they were investigating.

Gaidamachuk was what you would describe as an organised serial killer. Not only did she have an unsuspecting husband and family but she also did research on her victims. She would monitor the home of a potential victim to see how many visitors they had. If a potential victim had numerous visitors she would cross them off her list and look for a more isolated target. The police interviewed 3,000 people during their investigation. A breakthrough came in 2010 when an elderly woman managed to escape from Gaidamachuk and go to the police with a description of the attacker. At long last the police were now aware that the killer they were looking for was a woman.

The final victim was 81 year-old Alexandra Povaritsyna.

Gaidamachuk had pretended to be a decorator to get access to Povaritsyna's home and then battered her to death. Neighbours of Povaritsyna were able to give a description of the 'decorator' though and Irina Gaidamachuk was eventually arrested. She confessed the murders to the police and said - "I did it for money. I just wanted to be a normal mum, but I had a craving for drink. My husband wouldn't give me money for vodka."

Irina's husband and friends were astonished by the revelation that she was a brutal serial killer. They couldn't believe it. Irina Gaidamachuk was sentenced to twenty years in prison for her crimes. It seemed to be an absurdly light sentence - not least to the relatives of her victims. This though was the maximum sentence for female criminals in Russia. Believe it or not, Irina Gaidamachuk was found to be completely sane when subjected to tests in custody. She has a veritable battery of nicknames in true crime circles. The best of these is simply Satan in a Skirt. She is also known as The She-wolf of Krasnoufimsk and The Maniac-woman from Sverdlovsk.

(8) BABA ANUJKA (Years Active Late 19th Century-1920s, Fifty+ Suspected Victims)

Baba Anujka was born in Romania in 1838. She tends to be known as The Witch of Vladimirovac in true crime lore. As a young woman, Anujka had an affair with an army officer but he abandoned her. Not only that but he gave her an STD too. This experience is said to have left her with a hatred of men. She did though later get married and have eleven children. Tragedy struck multiple times though and only one of the children actually survived childhood.

Baba Anujka eventually became interested in herbalism and came up with an idea for a way to make money. She made her own 'love potions' which she sold to women who had unhappy marriages. Baba Anujka told the women that if they gave their husbands these potions the husband would become madly in love with them again and never be unfaithful. The love potions were marketed as 'magic water'. As this was an age where quack doctors flourished, Baba Anujka did a roaring trade in these bogus love potions and soon had many female customers eager to try them on their wayward and disinterested husbands.

There was only one problem though. The love potions, unknown to the women, were festooned with arsenic and toxins. Baba Anujka was not really interested in saving marriages. She was more interested in killing men. How many men died as a result of Baba Anujka's love potions? The true figure is impossible to verify but some estimates place the victim count at 150. At the very least it is believed that Baba Anujka killed fifty men with her deadly home brewed potions. Her murderous ruse came to an end when a woman named Stana Momirov had relatives die as a result of the potions and was arrested on suspicion of poisoning. Momirov told the authorities that she had got the potions from Baba Anujka.

Anujka was actually acquitted at her first trial in 1915 but she was later arrested again in 1928 when more evidence against her came to light. She was around 90 years-old when she was arrested - which must surely make her a strong contender for the oldest serial killer at the time of capture. Baba Anujka was sentenced to fifteen years in prison at her second trial. The lightish sentence was probably a consequence of the fact that they only had enough evidence to pin two murders on her. She was released on medical grounds eight years later and died in 1938 at the ripe old age of 100. This little old lady didn't look like much of a threat to anyone but purely in statistical terms she was one of the most prolific serial killers of all time.

(7) JUANA BARRAZA (Years Active 1998–2006, 40+ Suspected Victims)

Juana Barraza was known as The Old Lady Killer. She murdered between 42 and 48 elderly woman before being captured in 2006. Barraza was born in Mexico in 1957. Life for Barraza as a child, as so often for serial killers, was no bed of roses. Her mother apparently gave Barraza away to a man (in exchange for some beer) who then sexually abused her and made her pregnant. Barraza had four children in all. When she grew up she actually became a wrestler nicknamed La Dama del Silencio (The Lady of Silence). Barraza wrestled on the amateur circuit and also worked as popcorn vendor. She had another sideline though that was altogether less endearing or lawful.

Barraza would offer to help elderly ladies carry their groceries and thus gain admittance to a number of houses. Once inside, she then strangle with the victim with anything to hand - including telephone cords. Barraza was amazingly calculating and careful in the fashion that she targeted these vulnerable victims. She would do research beforehand to check that they lived alone and she had fake ID that suggested she was a nurse. Barraza would often pretend she had visited to check the blood pressure of the victim.

One of the confusing things about the murders from the police perspective was that they didn't seem to be financially motivated. Quite often the only thing missing from the houses of the victims was a small religious trinket (this was obviously the 'memento' of choice for Barraza when it came to keepsakes of her murders). Because Barraza was a powerful and strong women (she was, lest we forget, a wrestler!) these old ladies were overpowered very quickly and stood no chance of fighting back.

The lack of any sexual violence further served to confuse the police - although for a time both they and the Mexican public still assumed that the killer must be male. Eyewitness accounts of a 'stocky' and strongly built person fleeing the scene added to the perception that a man was responsible. When the police heard eyewitness accounts of a person fleeing the scene of a murder in female clothing they even questioned some known transvestites!

It's safe to say that the police involved in this case were not
Columbo. They took a long time to work out what was actually
happening. Dozens of victims fell to Barraza in her eight year
killng spree. At the start of 2006, Juana Barraza strangled an
82 year-old woman named Ana María de los Reyes Alfaro with
a stephoscope. However, someone discovered the body of the
victim almost straight away and contacted the police. Because
of the speed at which this all happened, Juana Barraza hadn't
had time to get out of the area and - matching the build of the
suspect in eyewitness accounts - she was arrested. The police
were rather gobsmacked to find that the killer was a woman.

Juana Barraza claimed she had visited the home of the last
victim to do some laundry (a likely story!) but soon buckled
and confessed to a few murders. The police accrued fingerprint
evidence that connected Juana Barraza to ten murders but
suspected her of over forty. Heaven knows how many people
she might actually have killed. In 2008, Juana Barraza was
sentenced to 759 years in prison. She showed no remorse for
her crimes and claimed she didn't act alone (the police
however found no evidence of any accomplices in these awful
murders). The motivation for the murders remains unclear but
Juana Barraza's painful childhood seemed to leave her with a
burning anger and bitterness which eventually manifested
itself in the most awful way imaginable.

(6) OLGA KONSTANTINOVA BRISCORN
(Years Active 1818–1822, 100+ Victims)

Olga Konstantinovna Briscorn was born in the Russian Empire
in 1776. She was a wealthy landowner and socialite who owned
numerous properties. She was also notorious for the cruel
manner in which she treated the serfs who worked for her.
Briscorn was responsible for much human misery and over a
hundred deaths. She was married to a provincial marshall and
this entitled her to hundreds of servants and a great deal of
wealth.

Olga was, on the surface, an interesting and respected woman. She loved the theatre and was said to be highly intelligent and witty. She also funded churches and temples and donated money to the poor. As Ichabod Crane might say though, villainy wears many masks - none so dangerous as the mask of virtue. Olga Konstantinovna Briscorn was what you might describe as a wolf in sheep's clothing.

After she was widowed, Briscorn married a diplomat and embarked on a bizarre double life. In St. Petersburg she was a kind and generous socialite but in the Dmitrievsky district of the Kursk Governorate, where she opened a cloth factory, she was an absolute monster. Life in this factory was grim to say the least. Workers were beaten with whips and starved to death. They were virtual prisoners in the factory and Olga Konstantinovna Briscorn would take away their property and force them to endure these slave labour conditions. A large number of people who died in the factory were only children.

When it was noted that the serf mortality rate had gone through the roof in the area thanks to the factory an investigation was launched but it took years to complete - during which time more serfs died. Many of the victims were buried in pits. Disease and starvation was allowed to run rampant in the factory and many serfs fled from the area in fear of being dragooned into employment at this horror factory. Those who were trapped in the factory had to work fifteen hour shifts. They barely slept and were constantly malnourished.

When the investigation was finished, Olga Konstantinovna Briscorn was removed as owner of the cloth factory and it was transferred into state ownership. You would have thought that she would get a much harsher sentence but the authorities were more concerned about fraud they'd uncovered at the factory than the deaths of all these serfs. Olga Konstantinovna Briscorn was therefore able to evade any serious charges and able to leave a sizeable fortune to her family when she died in

1836.

(5) MADAME POPOVA (Years Active 1879-1909, Hundreds of Suspected Victims)

Not much is known about the background or true age of Katharina Popova but we do know she came from Samara - a city in southwestern Russia, framed by the Volga and Samara rivers. Motivated by her own unhappy marriage, Popova set up a service whereby she would rid unhappy women of unwanted husbands by murdering them! Believe it or not, this business (which was obviously operated on a secret need to know basis) flourished for thirty years and claimed hundreds of victims.

Popova is said to have participated in many of the murders herself by engineering an acquaintance with the husband and then slipping him some arsenic. On other occasions a hitman was sometimes dispatched to do away with the husband in question. If you wanted to get rid of a husband and employed Popova you had to pay her half the fee up front and then the other half once the murder was completed. A surprisingly high number of women took advantage of this unusual and lethal business to get rid of husbands.

The highly successful if unorthodox business run by Katharina Popova came an end when a woman who paid for her husband to be murdered felt such dreadful remorse and guilt over the death that she went to the authorities and told them all about Popova and what had happened. When word got out about Popova's activities an angry mob descended and would have been perfectly happy to lynch her. Popova was calm though despite her capture. She said she was proud of what she had done and felt great pride in liberating hundreds of women from unhappy marriages.

Popova also proudly declared that she had never killed a single woman and that all the victims were men (as if that somehow excused her crimes! - they were ONLY men). Popova also seemed to be under the deluded belief that her murders had been very humane because she used or supplied poison. I'm fairly sure the person being poisoned didn't find it very humane! Popova had to be escorted to prison by armed soldiers to keep the unruly mob at bay. She was executed by firing squad in March 1909.

(4) AMELIA DYER (Years Active 1880–1896, Six Verified Victims, 400 Suspected Victims)

Amelia Dyer was born near Bristol in 1838. Dyer became known as the Reading Baby Farmer and the Angel Maker for her horrendous crimes in Victorian England. Dyer worked as a 'baby farmer' - this involved looking after illegitimate babies in the hope that someone might adopt them one day. Dyer deduced though that she could keep all the money she was paid to do this for herself if she just killed the babies and didn't have to spend money on food, clothes, medicine, and bedding. It is estimated that she killed 400 babies. Amelia Dyer was plainly one of the most evil and cold hearted people that ever lived.

Dyer was a nurse as a young woman but she struggled financially. Through other nurses she became aware of 'baby farming' - where women were paid to look after babies who were awaiting adoption. One of Dyer's adverts went like this - 'I should be glad to have a dear little baby girl, one I could bring up and call my own. First I must tell you we are plain, homely people, in fairly good circumstances. We live in our own house. I have a good and comfortable home. We are out in the country and sometimes I am alone a good deal. I do not want a child for money's sake but for company and home comfort. Myself and my husband are dearly fond of children. I have no child of my own. A child with me will have a good home and a mother's love and care. We belong to the Church of England. Although I want to bring the child up as my own, I should not mind the mother or any other person coming to see the child at any time. It would be a satisfaction to see and know the child was getting on all right. I only hope we can come to terms.'

Dyer struggled financially when her (much older) husband died and she became mentally unstable because she was addicted to opium. She deduced that if she simply let babies starve to death she could save a lot of money for herself. The authorities became suspicious of Dyer but she negated this by moving around the country a lot so that the scrutiny on her was never too localised or specific. At one point she was sentenced to hard labour for neglecting a baby but after she was released she simply went back to her old wicked ways.

In 1895 she moved to Reading but babies began to be found in the Thames river. One of the babies had a name and address tag that was connected to Dyer. Dyer had started dumping babies in the river so that she could avoid having to get a death certificate (which naturally might mean a medical examination of the deceased babies). Dyer was arrested in 1896. Dyer's defence team pleaded insanity on her behalf at the Old Bailey. One of her last acts in prison was to write a confession denying that she had accomplices. Her main motivation was to protect her daughter (who was suspected of being in league with her mother when it came to the deaths).

'I feel my days are numbered on this earth,' wrote Dyer, 'but I do feel it is an awful thing drawing innocent people into trouble I do know I shal [sic] have to answer before my Maker in Heaven for the awful crimes I have committed but as God Almighty is my judge in Heaven on Hearth neither my daughter Mary Ann Palmer nor her husband Alfred Ernest Palmer I do most solemnly declare neither of them had any thing [sic] at all to do with it, they never knew I contemplated doing such a wicked thing until it was too late I am speaking the truth and nothing but the truth as I hope to be forgiven, I myself and I alone must stand before my Maker in Heaven to give an answer for it all witness my hand, Amelia Dyer.'

On Wednesday the 10th of June 1896, Amelia Dyer was

hanged by James Billington at Newgate prison. The case of Amelia Dyer made Victorian England rethink the policy of 'baby farming' and introduce stricter laws when it came to foster care and adoption. Dyer's insanity was difficult to predict though because she was a trained nurse and someone who seemed (on the face of it) perfectly qualified to look after babies. Because Amelia Dyer was active around the same time as Jack the Ripper, there is a very speculative (and rather outlandish) theory she might have been responsible for the Jack the Ripper murders. While that seems unlikely, there is no question that Amelia Dyer was one of the most heartless killers who ever lived.

(3) DELFINA AND MARIA DE JESUS GONZALEZ (Years Active 1950s-1963, 90+ Suspected Victims)

Delfina and María de Jesús González were Mexican sisters born in El Salto de Juanacatlan, Jalisco. Life was pretty tough for the sisters growing up. Their father would apparently have them locked up in the local jail if they misbehaved as children! One thing the sisters really hated was the poverty they experienced as children. They had a burning desire to escape from that poverty and never experience it again in their adult lives. This desire imbued in them a ruthless streak (to put it mildly). These were two tough women who had no moral compass when it came to ambition and money. They would do literally anything necessary to earn a crust.

Delfina and María were also helped in their crimes by two other sisters named Carmen and Maria Luisa. While the latter were a part of the crimes that followed it was Delfina and María who remained the focal point and became infamous. From 1945 until 1964, the sisters ran Rancho El Ángel. This was the hub of a prostitution ring. The sisters had started out running a bar but deduced that prostitution was way more lucrative. The sisters had brothels in San Francisco del Rincon Purisima del Rincon, Leon in Guanajuato state, El Salto and

San Juan de los Lagos, Jalisco, San Juan del Rio, and
Queretaro state. These brothels required hundreds of 'working
girls' and it transpired that the sisters were not employer of
the year material. Quite the contrary.

These establishments were run more like prisons than
brothels. In 1964, a young woman named Catalina Ortega
stumbled into a police station in Guanajuato. Catalina had
visible injuries and had clearly been through a dreadful ordeal.
She told the police that the Gonzalez sisters were running the
local brothel as it was a concentration camp and that awful
things had happened there. When the police went to search
the brothel for evidence of this alarming tale they found eighty
female bodies, eleven male bodies, and several fetuses. The
Gonzalez sisters had been killing girls who were no longer fit
for work and if any prostitute got pregnant they would kill the
child.

The working girls at the brothel (who had applied to adverts
looking for maids) were kept like slaves and forcibly hooked
on drugs to make them compliant. Girls at the brothel were
not allowed to go outside, locked in rooms, and sometimes
starved to death. Rancho El Ángel literally was the brothel
from hell. It was worse than any horror film you could
imagine. It wasn't just prostitutes who were murdered. The
Gonzalez sisters would also kill rich male clients at the brothel
so they could rob them.

'Once these gals entered the brothel,' wrote CulturecrossFire,
'they were held as prisoners, some never even able to go
outside. Virgins who were brought in were set-aside for special
customers who paid higher rates to deflower the girls. None of
the women ever saw a dime for their dreadful duties. Business
boomed and the ring of whorehouses spread to Mexico City
and several other areas. The only set back came when biology
got in the way and the girls started to become pregnant. This
led to forcible back alley style abortions, with the babies being
buried on the property. Eventually when the sex slaves grew
ill, suffered from an STD or just stopped being willing to

perform, they too were murdered and buried on the land surrounding the brothels. The killings were not done in a humane way either, as women were intentionally starved to death by being placed in locked rooms. Others were bludgeoned with logs. Even some customers never found their way out of the whorehouse if they happened to show off too much money. In those cases the men were killed, then robbed and buried.'

Catalina Ortega, who managed to tell the police about the sisters, had barely escaped with her life. The Gonzalez sisters and their cronies had been trying to find her so they could kill her. When he Gonzalez sisters were arrested and word got out of what they had been doing in these brothels an angry lynch mob soon gathered. The González sisters were each sentenced to forty years in prison. Delfina died behind bars but María actually lived long enough to be released. The story of the Gonzalez sisters was a complex and macabre tale. They had caused unimaginable human misery and were responsible for many deaths through their ruthless brothel businesses. It is believed that the four sisters potentially killed more than 150 people or even more than 200 people. This would make the Gonzalez sisters, as a collective, among the most prolific killers of all time.

(2) GIULIA TOFANA (Years Active 1633-1651, 600 Alleged Victims)

Giulia Tofana was born in 1620 in Palermo. Tofana was the daughter of Thofania d'Amado - a woman who was executed for murdering her own husband. It is said that a few secrets on how to bump off men were passed down from mother to daughter. Giulia Tofana was a legendary poisoner who is alleged to have clocked up 600 victims (though this is unverifiable as records from the time are naturally difficult to get hold of and barely exist). Giulia Tofana was what you might call a forerunner of Katharina Popova in that she offered a service whereby she would help unhappy wives kill their husbands. Giulia had a cosmetics product called Aqua Tofana which was essentially supposed to be an ointment for bad skin. This product however contained arsenic and other dangerous elements which meant it could be used as a poison. It was a clever way to disguise the method of murder for these wives.

'Another element of Giulia's poison that made it so masterfully deceitful is how it killed its victims,' wrote Syfy. 'The first dose, normally diluted with some kind of liquid, would cause exhaustion and physical weakness. The second dose would bring on stomach aches, vomiting, and dysentery. The third or fourth dose would take care of the rest. The poison, and the method of administering it, meant that doctors and investigators believed the death had been caused by some unknown illness or disease. The slow-nature of the poisoning meant that victims had a chance to get their affairs in order, and their wives were there to exert their influence over what that order looked like. And the deaths — those tragically young lives lost to their sickbeds — were never believed to be anything more. The poison undetectable, the murders free of suspicion, Giulia's business flourished.'

Giulia Tofana's daughter Girolama Spera was also a willing accomplice in this deadly scheme. The story goes that Giulia Tofana was caught when a wife put this deadly beauty product in her husband's soup but then had second thoughts and told him not to eat it. When he learned what was going on, the woman's husband made her go to the authorities and rat on Giulia Tofana. Tofana was given refuge in a local church at first but when a (false) rumour spread that she had poisoned the water supply in Rome she was arrested and tortured. Giulia Tofana confessed to six hundred murders but this figure is impossible to substantiate. We do know though that her activities were responsible for an awful lot of deaths. It is believed that Giulia Tofana and her daughter were executed. Their bodies were thrown from the church that had given them shelter. It is sometimes reported that the composer Mozart was killed by means of Aqua Tofana but this is believed to be an urban myth.

(1) ELIZABETH BATHORY (Years Active 1590–1610, 600+ Suspected Victims)

The most prolific female serial killer was Elizabeth Báthory (aka Countess Elizabeth Báthory de Ecsed). She was born in Nyírbátor, Kingdom of Hungary, in 1560, and a Hungarian noblewoman from the rich family of Báthory. Elizabeth Báthory was notoriously cruel and wicked though. The source of this wickedness is still open to speculation. She is said to have suffered seizures as a child. Báthory also grew up witnessing executions - which is obviously not something that is going to have a tremendously positive effect on anyone.

The Báthory family ruled Transylvania as an independent principality. Elizabeth Báthory was married at fourteen and had numerous lovers. Báthory's main hobby seemed to be torturing young girls who served at her castle as servants. Witnesses claimed that she would stab victims or burn them. She is also alleged to have bitten victims and starved them to death. It is said that Elizabeth Báthory believed that the only way to stay youthful was to drink the blood of young virgins. The legend of Elizabeth Báthory often depicts her taking a bath in the blood of her victims but this is usually considered to be an embellishment that was added to the legend years after her death.

Elizabeth Báthory is often depicted as a vampire (or at the very least someone who practised vampirism) but this is not something that as ever verified (in so far as you can ever verify anything that happened so long ago). The Hungarian authorities, as you might expect, eventually heard tales of some very nutty stuff going on at the home of Elizabeth Báthory so they decided to investigate. In 1610 they arrested Elizabeth Báthory and also a number of servant girls who were judged to have been accomplices in the grisly affairs going on. The servants were executed but Elizabeth Báthory's noble blood saved her from this fate.

Elizabeth Báthory did not go unpunished though. Far from it. Elizabeth Báthory was made a solitary prisoner of Csetje Castle - where the windows were walled up so that she could not gaze upon daylight. She died there at the age of 54 in 1614. She tends to be known as The Blood Countess today in true crime articles. Seperating fact from fiction in the story of Elizabeth Báthory is not easy but we do know that the investigation provided a number of eyewitnesses who testified to her wickedness. 300 witnesses gave accounts of various unpleasant methods of torture favoured by Báthory.

The torture methods included ironing the feet of people, stitching lips together, making people stand in ice until they froze to death, jamming pins and needles under the fingernails, lacerating genitals, and strangling people with scarves, covering people with honey and allowing them to (gulp) be attacked by bees, and making people cook and eat their own flesh. Báthory never actually got to mount a defence or have a proper trial though. It was a rather one-sided affair where the outcome was never likely to be in doubt. Some of the legend of Báthory is folklore and some of it is true. It's safe to say though that employment at Elizabeth Báthory's house was probably the worst job in the world. You had about as much life expectancy as a soldier in the trenches of World War I.

Elizabeth Báthory was clearly an influence on Dracula. She is a classic example of how power can corrupt. Elizabeth Báthory thought that her noble blood gave her the right to do anything she wanted to - however wicked. She is still credited as being the worst female killer of all time in terms of pure statistics.